UK Nature Conservation No. 25

Seabird numbers and breeding success
in Britain and Ireland, 2000

R.A. Mavor, G. Pickerell, M. Heubeck & K.R. Thompson.

Roddy Mavor and Kate Thompson, Seabird Monitoring Programme, Seabirds and Cetaceans, Joint Nature Conservation Committee, Dunnet House, 7 Thistle Place, Aberdeen, AB10 1UZ

Georgina Pickerell, Research Department, Royal Society for the Protection of Birds, The Lodge, Sandy, Bedfordshire, SG19 2DL

Martin Heubeck, Shetland Oil Terminal Environmental Advisory Group, Department of Zoology, University of Aberdeen, Tillydrone Avenue, Aberdeen, AB9 2TN

Cover painting of kittiwakes by David Bennett.
Cover design by Green Associates, 1994.

Further information on JNCC publications can be obtained from:
JNCC, Monkstone House, City Road, Peterborough PE1 1JY

Published by Joint Nature Conservation Committee, Peterborough

ISBN 1 86107 533 2

ISSN 0963 8083

This report should be cited as follows:

Mavor, R.A., Pickerell, G., Heubeck, M. & Thompson, K.R. 2001. *Seabird numbers and breeding success in Britain and Ireland, 2000.* Peterborough, Joint Nature Conservation Committee. (UK Nature Conservation, No. 25.)

Contents

Summary

This report presents the results of monitoring of seabird populations and breeding success throughout Britain and Ireland in 2000 and makes comparisons with previous years. The report is produced annually as part of the JNCC's Seabird Monitoring Programme, in collaboration with the Royal Society for the Protection of Birds (RSPB) and the Shetland Oil Terminal Environmental Advisory Group (SOTEAG). Some findings of particular note in 2000 are summarised below:

- A June storm had a severe impact on west facing colonies in Shetland and Orkney, affecting a wide range of species (red-throated diver, Northern gannet, European shag, Arctic skua, mew gull, herring gull, black-legged kittiwake, Arctic tern, and common and black guillemots). At Sumburgh Head, it was estimated that the storm killed thousands of common guillemot chicks and washed away 75% of European shag nests.

- The rapid decline of black-legged kittiwake populations continues. In Shetland, breeding success was poor for the third season in four years, with the severe June storm and predation contributing at some colonies to difficulties caused by apparent food shortages. Whole colony counts revealed declines at Fair Isle (-30% since 1997), Noss (-17% since 1998) and on Foula (-11% since 1999). In Orkney, numbers at Mull Head and Costa Head have fallen by 35% since 1997.

- In Shetland, numbers of Northern fulmars continue to increase at monitored study plots. However, whole colony counts of Fair Isle and Foula revealed declines of over 50% since 1996 and 1987 respectively.

- A census of Leach's storm-petrel on the St Kilda archipelago revealed a total of almost 43,000 apparently occupied sites. Dun held 65% of the birds, Boreray 24%, Hirta 6% and Soay 5%.

- Predators continued to have an effect on several species. Despite ongoing control measures, mink continue to reduce productivity at some gull and tern colonies in west Scotland. Predation by foxes caused 75% nest failure at the Orford Ness gull colony. On Fair Isle, domestic cats are thought to be responsible for the desertion of several traditional black guillemot sites. Productivity at several tern colonies was reduced due to predation by common buzzard, common kestrel, herring gull and fox. After a successful rat eradication programme on Handa, Atlantic puffins are recolonising a former breeding site.

- In Orkney, Arctic skua and great skua declined on Hoy and on Papa Westray. However, both species increased on Handa. Predation of Arctic skua chicks by great skuas was a problem at several Shetland sites.

- The largest British great black-backed gull colony on Hoy declined further, down 25% since 1996.

- At the mixed gull colony on South Walney, an outbreak of botulism caused significant mortality for the third successive year. Botulism also caused notable mortality among herring gull chicks on Ynysoedd Gwylan, near Bardsey, and among great black-backed gull chicks on Sanda.

- Range extensions were noted for two species. Great skuas nested on Canna for the first time. Black guillemots bred on Ynys Gwylan Fawr, near Bardsey, after an apparent spread from Anglesey.

- Northern gannet numbers increased on Foula by 20% since 1994. On Grassholm, analysis of photographs of the gannetry taken in 1999, together with a ground check done in 2000, revealed a 10% increase in numbers since 1994 and confirmed the presence of a new sub-colony.

- Overall numbers of great cormorants declined in the north and east, but increased in the south and west. Numbers of European shags increased in most regions; these increases were particularly striking along North Sea coasts where marked declines in numbers of pairs attempting to breed had been noted in 1999.

- Mediterranean gull data were received from six sites, which held a total of 68-69 pairs.

- Breeding success was good for most tern species though Arctic tern and little tern productivity was below the level required to maintain their breeding populations.

- Breeding success for razorbills was below average at all colonies.

1 Introduction

This is the twelfth annual report on the results of seabird monitoring at colonies throughout Britain and Ireland, produced jointly by JNCC, RSPB and SOTEAG, as part of JNCC's Seabird Monitoring Programme. Available data on seabird breeding numbers and breeding success at seabird colonies in 2000 are summarised and compared with results from previous years, primarily 1999.

The information contained in this report has been collated from many sources. These include: research staff and wardens from a variety of organisations including RSPB, SOTEAG, JNCC, Scottish Natural Heritage, English Nature, Countryside Council for Wales, Irish National Parks and Wildlife Service, the Wildlife Trusts, bird observatories, National Trust and National Trust for Scotland, the Centre for Ecology and Hydrology and BirdWatch Ireland. Many dedicated fieldwork volunteers also contribute valuable data to the Seabird Monitoring Programme; refer to the Acknowledgements section for details.

One aim of the annual report is to draw attention to notable changes in seabird numbers or breeding success which may merit direct conservation action or further research. It is also intended to provide feedback and, we hope, encouragement for future work, to the many individuals and organisations contributing data, by placing results for individual colonies or regions in a wider context The results presented refer mainly to coastal or island populations of seabirds, but reference is also made to inland populations of great cormorants, gulls and terns where data are available.

Any comments on this report, or offers of help for future seasons, would be greatly appreciated by the authors. We are also keen to receive any existing additional information on numbers or breeding success for any seabird species, whether at coastal or inland colonies, that may not have been previously submitted to the Seabird Monitoring Programme. Any such data will be added to the long-term seabird databases maintained by JNCC and RSPB, including the JNCC/Seabird Group's Seabird Colony Register.

Details of recommended methods for assessing seabird numbers and breeding success are given in the *Seabird monitoring handbook for Britain and Ireland* (Walsh *et al.* 1995). Copies of the *Handbook*, or other advice on seabird monitoring methodology, may be obtained from the Seabirds and Cetaceans Unit of JNCC at the address given on the title page.

1.1 The Seabird Monitoring Programme and Seabird Colony Register

The JNCC's Seabird Monitoring Programme facilitates the co-ordination of seabird monitoring on a UK-wide basis. The aim of the programme is to ensure that sufficient data on breeding numbers and breeding performance of seabirds are collected both regionally and nationally to enable their conservation status to be assessed. The programme assists JNCC, RSPB and partner organisations, including the statutory country agencies, to monitor aspects of the health of the wider marine environment and to provide sound advice relevant to the conservation needs of breeding seabirds.

Seabird monitoring directly funded by JNCC focuses particularly on species such as Northern fulmar, European shag, black-legged kittiwake and auks, for which changes in breeding populations, breeding success or other parameters may provide evidence of changes in the marine environment as a whole. The most detailed monitoring is undertaken, through external contracts, at several geographically dispersed 'key sites': Isle of May (south-east Scotland), Fair Isle (Shetland), Canna (north-west Scotland) and Skomer (Wales). Long-term monitoring of numbers and breeding success is also undertaken on Orkney Mainland, on St. Kilda (north-west Scotland) and in Grampian (north-east Scotland). Monitoring of breeding success of cliff-breeding species is also encouraged by JNCC at many other colonies, partly by contributing to fieldwork costs of volunteers via the Seabird Group.

The RSPB monitors the numbers and breeding success of a range of seabird species throughout the UK through their network of reserves, and largely co-ordinates the monitoring of terns in Britain. Further RSPB monitoring or survey effort is directed at petrels and skuas.

In Shetland, Aberdeen University, under contract to SOTEAG, carries out extensive population monitoring of cliff-nesting species and black guillemots. This work is funded by the Sullom Voe Association Ltd., and forms part of a wider scheme of biological monitoring in Shetland. For Northern fulmar, common guillemot and razorbill, annual counts are carried out in sample plots, while for European shag, black-legged kittiwake and black guillemot, counts are made of longer stretches of coastline at intervals of two or more years. Breeding success has also been assessed annually at many colonies since the mid-1980s.

Available data for Irish colonies are also collated by JNCC and RSPB, helping to place patterns or trends for British colonies in a wider context. Contacts are maintained with a number of bodies, including the National Parks and Wildlife Service and BirdWatch Ireland. Fieldwork at some Irish colonies is grant-aided by the Seabird Group.

The JNCC and Seabird Group also collaborate on the Seabird Colony Register, a database of colony counts for Britain and Ireland for the period 1969 to 1998, which is maintained as part of the Seabird Monitoring Programme. Many observers and organisations (including SOTEAG and RSPB) have contributed to the SCR and data have also been abstracted from sources such as research reports and county bird reports. Nearly all coastal colonies in Britain and Ireland were censused for the SCR in 1985-87, providing a baseline for seabird populations. Population changes since the previous complete survey (the Seabird Group's Operation Seafarer in 1969-70) are summarised in Table 1.1. A repeat census of British and Irish seabird colonies, Seabird 2000 (running from 1999-2002), is currently under way and a new seabird colony database for the period from 1999 is being developed within the National Biodiversity Network framework.

1.2 Data presentation and methods

Some potential limitations of the information presented are outlined below. Further discussion of methodological considerations and details of analyses are given in the *Seabird monitoring handbook* (Walsh *et al.* 1995) and in previous annual reports.

1.2.1 Population changes: use of regional samples

In order to allow concise and standardised presentation of population data, individual colonies are generally not considered in detail in this report. Details of the original counts used in assessing population changes are held by JNCC, RSPB and SOTEAG.

For most species, with the exception of some terns, it is neither practicable nor valid to assess year-to-year changes for the breeding population as a whole, because such changes may vary markedly between different areas and monitoring effort is uneven. Instead, the coastline has been subdivided into 14 'regions', as defined in Figure 1.1 and Table 1.2. Within each region, valid counts of whole colonies (excluding very small colonies and colonies where counting error is known or suspected to exceed 5%), or of sample plots within colonies, are summed for year-to-year population comparisons. The aim of this approach is to draw attention to any common patterns shown by a number of regions, as well as to highlight any notable changes shown by colonies in particular regions.

Regional population changes for most species are tabulated for 1999 and 2000. Some of the changes indicated by these counts may be of a short-term nature, not necessarily indicative of longer-term trends, e.g. year-to-year changes in species such as black-legged kittiwake or European shag may in some instances reflect fluctuations in the proportion of the adult population attempting to breed. Movements of breeding birds to or from unmonitored colonies, notably in the case of terns, great cormorants, and black-headed gulls, may also contribute to apparent changes. Even where inter-colony movements do not occur, changes shown by sample populations are not necessarily representative of wider populations.

Table 1.1 Counts or estimates of total breeding populations of seabirds in Britain and Ireland. Most figures are for 1985-87 (Lloyd *et al.* 1991) but those for Northern gannet, skuas, Mediterranean gull, roseate tern and Arctic tern include more recent updates. Figures for Britain exclude the Isle of Man and the Channel Islands (included under Britain & Ireland). For population estimates for Great Britain (excluding the Isle of Man) and UK (GB plus Northern Ireland) see Stone *et al.* (1997). Units are 'pairs' for most species (apparently occupied nests/sites or, for skuas, territories), with the exception of auks, for which units are individual birds ('i' in table).

	Coastal population		% change[2]	Total population[3]	
	Britain	Britain & Ireland[1]	1969-87 B & I coast	Britain	Britain & Ireland[1]
Northern fulmar	537,000	571,000	+85%	537,000	571,000
Manx shearwater[4]	*c.* 235,000	*c.* 275,000	?	*c.* 235,000	*c.* 275,000
European storm-petrel	41+ colonies	72+ colonies	?	41+ cols.	72+ cols.
Leach's storm-petrel	6+ colonies	7+ colonies	?	6+ cols.	7+ cols.
Northern gannet[5]	206,700	242,900	+36%	206,700	242,900
Great cormorant	6,000	10,400	+30%	6,800	11,700
European shag	36,400	47,300	+40%	36,400	47,300
Arctic skua[6]	3,100	3,100	≤ +220%	3,100	3,100
Great skua[6]	8,800	8,800	≤ +150%	8,800	8,800
Mediterranean gull[7]	63	64	≥ +200%	64	65
Black-headed gull	77,300	84,200	+13%	167,000	233,000
Mew gull	14,800	15,700	+21%	67,800	71,400
Lesser black-backed gull	62,300	65,700	+31%	82,300	88,700
Herring gull	135,000	191,000	-43%	150,000	206,000
Great black-backed gull	18,300	23,300	+3%	18,400	23,400
Black-legged kittiwake	492,000	544,000	+22%	492,000	544,000
Sandwich tern	14,000	18,400	+53%	14,000	18,600
Roseate tern[8]	50	>750	-80%	50	>750
Common tern	11,800	14,700	-1%	12,700	16,000
Arctic tern[9]	42,400	44,900	-14%	42,900	45,500
Little tern	2,400	2,800	+40%	2,400	2,800
Common guillemot	1,047,000i	1,203,000i	+118%	1,047,000i	1,203,000I
Razorbill	147,000i	182,000i	Probably +	147,000i	182,000I
Black guillemot	37,500i	40,500i	Probably +	37,500i	40,500I
Atlantic puffin[10]	898,000i	940,000i	Slightly +?	898,000i	940,000I

Notes:

1. Irish figures include some estimates (mainly for Northern fulmar, European shag and gulls) for coastal sections which had not been surveyed by 1988.
2. Net change based on comparison with total recorded during the 1969-70 'Operation Seafarer' survey (reanalysis of counts summarised by Cramp *et al.* 1974); differences in count methods prevent direct comparison for some species.
3. British & Irish totals for some species include estimates of inland populations.
4. Manx shearwater figures are very approximate (midpoints of population estimates).
5. Northern gannet figures are from a complete survey of North Atlantic colonies carried out in 1994 and 1995 (Murray & Wanless 1997) with updates for colonies counted subsequently.
0. Skua figures are from the 1992 surveys of Orkney and Shetland (Meek *et al.* 1994; Sears *et al.* 1995), with a 1996 update for Hoy (Furness 1997), otherwise 1985-87 with updates to 1996 for Handa and St. Kilda. Although some nest inland in mainland Scotland, all are treated as coastal here.
0. Mediterranean gull figures are from Ogilvie *et al.* 2000.
8. Roseate tern figures are from 2000 (this report).
9. Arctic tern figures include Shetland and Orkney counts from the 1989 RSPB survey (Avery *et al.* 1993), with counts of individuals divided by 1.5 to give an estimate of pairs.
10. Atlantic puffin figures are very approximate, and include a high proportion of counts of pairs multiplied by two to give estimates of numbers of individuals.

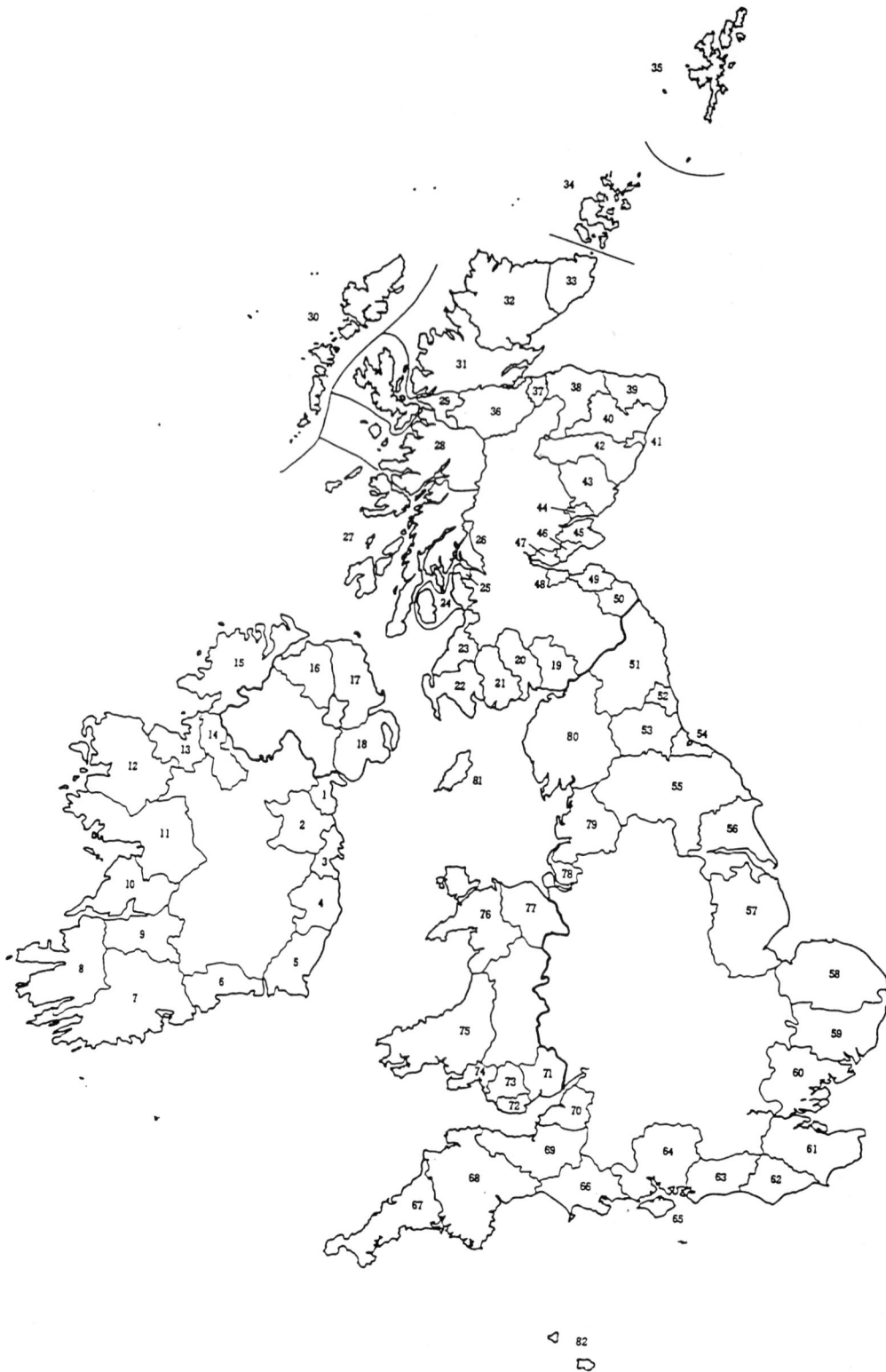

Figure 1.1 Coastal counties and districts of Britain and Ireland. See Table 1.2 for details of the coastal regions (combinations of counties or districts) used in this report. Reproduced, with permission, from Lloyd *et al.* (1991).

Table 1.2 Groupings of coastal counties and districts used in assessing regional population changes. These regions are based on Figure 2 of Lloyd *et al.* (1991), except that Shetland and Orkney are each treated separately from 'NE Scotland' and the Inverness to Caithness coastline is treated separately ('N Scotland') from 'NW Scotland'.

County or district name (numbers refer to Figure 1.1)	Region
Louth (1), Meath (2), Dublin (3), Wicklow (4), Wexford (5), Waterford (6)	SE Ireland
Cork (7), Kerry (8), Limerick (9), Clare (10)	SW Ireland
Galway (11), Mayo (12), Sligo (13), Leitrim (14), Donegal (15)	NW Ireland
Londonderry (16), Antrim (17), Down (18)	NE Ireland
Annandale & Eskdale (19), Nithsdale (20), Stewartry (21), Wigtown (22), Kyle & Carrick (23), Cunninghame (24), Inverclyde (25), Dunbarton (26), Argyll & Bute (27)	SW Scotland
Lochaber (28), Skye & Lochalsh (29), Western Isles (30), west coast of Ross & Cromarty (31), north-west coast of Sutherland (32)	NW Scotland
Orkney (34)	Orkney
Shetland (35)	Shetland
Caithness (33), east coast of Sutherland (32), east coast of Ross & Cromarty (31), Inverness (32)	N Scotland
Nairn (37), Moray (38), Banff & Buchan (39), Gordon (40), City of Aberdeen (41), Kincardine & Deeside (42)	NE Scotland
Angus (43), City of Dundee (44), north-east Fife (45), Kirkcaldy (46), Dunfermline (47), West Lothian, City of Edinburgh (48), East Lothian (49), Berwickshire (50)	SE Scotland
Northumberland (51), Tyne & Wear (52), Durham (53), Cleveland (54), North Yorkshire (55), Humberside (56), Lincolnshire (57)	NE England
Norfolk (58), Suffolk (59), Essex (60)	E England
Kent (61), East Sussex (62), West Sussex (63), Hampshire (64), Isle of Wight (65)	SE England
Dorset (66), Cornwall & Isles of Scilly (67), Devon (68), Somerset (69), Avon (70), Gloucestershire, Channel Islands (82)	SW England and Channel Islands
Gwent (71), South Glamorgan (72), Mid Glamorgan (73), West Glamorgan (74), Dyfed (75), Gwynedd (76), Clwyd (77)	Wales
Merseyside (78), Lancashire (79), Cumbria (80), Isle of Man (81)	NW England and Isle of Man

1.2.2 Calculation of population trends

Regional population trends are assessed using population indices, rather than sums of actual colony counts, because different combinations of colonies may be counted in different years. The population index in a baseline year (1986 unless otherwise noted), is set at 100, subsequent population changes being expressed relative to this value. Further details of the derivation of these population indices are given in Walsh *et al.* (1990) and in Thompson *et al.* (1997).

Average annual rates of population change are calculated by linear regression of the logarithms of index values on year. The significance of the slope of the regression, equivalent to the average annual rate of increase or decrease in the population, is then assessed using the t-test (Wilkinson 1990). Population trends are not presented in this report for some mobile species, such as gulls, Arctic terns and common terns, for which the numbers of colonies and/or breeding pairs monitored each year are considered too small to enable wider population trends to be confidently assessed.

1.2.3 Accuracy and representativeness of counts

In comprehensive assessments of long-term changes in seabird numbers, e.g. between 1969-70 and 1985-87 (Lloyd *et al.* 1991), there is inevitably some loss of count accuracy at the expense of obtaining complete geographical coverage. However, stricter criteria, covering factors such as census unit, timing, frequency and apparent accuracy of counts, need to be applied when selecting counts for assessment of short-term changes, as in this report. For most species, single, well-timed counts of apparently occupied nests are sufficient. However, the possibility of undetected variations in count accuracy, count coverage or timing of breeding season should be borne in mind.

For Northern fulmar, common guillemot and razorbill, numbers of adults attending colonies can fluctuate markedly from day to day. Given this source of variation, assessment of population change for these species ideally requires five to ten counts of adults (auks) or apparently occupied nest-sites (fulmars) in June each year. The statistical significance of changes shown by such counts can be assessed using t-tests. Where such replication of counts is necessary, it is rarely possible to count the whole of a large colony. Therefore, counts are usually of sample plots within a colony, but these plots, even where randomly selected, will not necessarily be representative of the colony as a whole.

The seabird colonies regularly monitored may not be representative of British or Irish populations as a whole. Representativeness is more likely to be achieved within particular regions, but cannot be assumed, especially if few colonies or small population samples are monitored. In particular, if efforts are concentrated on individual colonies, the formation of new colonies elsewhere may go undetected. Coverage of extensive stretches of coastline is a more satisfactory approach for species not requiring replicate counts. This approach is used, for example, in SOTEAG's monitoring of European shags, black-legged kittiwakes and black guillemots in Shetland.

1.2.4 Breeding success: use of 'low-input' methods

For general monitoring purposes, the number of chicks fledged per breeding pair is the most useful parameter for gauging breeding success. Productivity of species other than terns is usually assessed for sample plots, ideally randomly selected, within colonies. For such species, the figures presented here have generally been averaged (rather than combined) across plots. For terns, whole-colony assessments of productivity are usually made. Full details of breeding success monitoring methods are given in Walsh *et al.* (1995). For some species or regions where few colonies are currently monitored, the results presented may not be fully representative. Also, in many cases, 'low-input' methods of assessing breeding success are used and these will tend to overestimate the productivity of breeding pairs slightly (Walsh *et al.* 1995). However, this is considered acceptable, as major geographical or year-to-year changes will still be obvious.

2　General features of the 2000 breeding season

In 2000, adverse weather conditions, especially during June, was a major factor in determining the fortunes of seabirds during the breeding season.

Apart from a brief anticyclonic spell between the 5th and 10th, April 2000 was dominated by low pressure. Northerly and easterly winds were frequent during the first half of the month, but southerlies prevailed after mid-month. Rainfall was high with many regions experiencing double the monthly average. For England and Wales as a whole it was the wettest April since 1756. Temperatures were around normal (Eden 2000a). The first half of May 2000 was dominated by a north-easterly airflow, after which an unsettled westerly type prevailed with vigorous troughs and depressions crossing the country at frequent intervals. A month of contrasts saw up to four times the normal May rainfall fall in south-east England while much of west Scotland, north-west England and northern Wales, and Northern Ireland recorded below average levels. Mean temperature was just above average (Eden 2000b). Red-throated divers and cormorants were noted nesting early at various sites in Shetland (Okill 2000a, Rodger 2000) and kittiwakes also bred early on the Isle of May.

In June 2000, low pressure controlled Britain's weather until the 13th, and from the 20th to 24th, with relatively high pressure prevailing at other times. A deepening Atlantic depression tracked north-eastwards between Scotland and Ireland during the 12th and 13th with its lowest central pressure of 968 mbar being the lowest in the region since June 1944. During this period winds averaged 40-50 knots in north and west Scotland, with gusts in excess of 70 knots, not only causing blocked roads and downed power lines but also setting a North Sea oil rig adrift. The mean June temperature in central England was warmer than average though most areas of Scotland were cooler than normal. Rainfall and sunshine percentages were variable (Eden 2000c). In early June, gales washed common guillemots and black-legged kittiwakes off lower cliffs on Skomer and heavy rain caused a land slip that destroyed some Atlantic puffin burrows (Brown & Easton 2000). In mid-June the storm during the 12th and 13th devastated south-west facing colonies at Sumburgh Head in Shetland. Thousands of common guillemot chicks were killed, and 75% of European shag nests were also washed away. On Foula, a few red-throated diver nests were flooded. The low productivity of Northern gannets at Hermaness may also have been caused by the storm, though the majority of failures occurred up to two weeks after the event (Rodger 2000). Weather conditions also had a serious effect on Arctic terns on Fetlar where no young fledged (Smith & Luxford 2000).

July 2000 was also dominated by low pressure until the 15th and again from the 25th until the end of the month. Most regions were dry and sunny between these dates and over much of Scotland and Northern Ireland it was the driest July in 100 years. Mean temperature was near normal in all areas except east England which was cooler than usual (Eden 2000d).

Limited data are available on feeding conditions. In Shetland, there appeared to be less availability of sandeels *Ammodytes* spp. than in 1999 (Heubeck 2000). It was a similar situation on Foula to that in 1999; great skua pellets again contained very few sandeels by early July, being replaced by whitefish (Furness 2000). In contrast, sandeel availability to black-legged kittiwakes and European shags appeared to be very good. On the Isle of May, breeding success of the two species with the highest reliance on sandeels (black-legged kittiwake and European shag) was well above the long-term average. High percentages of sandeels were recorded in the diets of both species, and to a lesser extent in the diets of three species of auk. For the first time since 1989 there was no commercial sandeel fishery on the Wee Bankie, an important feeding ground for seabirds lying *c.*30km east of the island, and it is possible that this was of benefit during the breeding season (Bull *et al.* 2000). On Canna in north-west Scotland, guillemot chick weights were again high. The diet was a typical mixture of sprats, sandeels and Gadidae, though the sandeels were significantly smaller than average due to a large number of '0'-group sandeels being taken (Swann 2000a). At Rockabill, indications were that food availability was good with sandeels predominating in the diet of roseate terns (Crowe *et al.* 2000).

3. Species accounts

Nomenclature follows *Checklist of Birds of Britain and Ireland* (BOU 1992) and subsequent relevant BOURC updates published in the journal *Ibis*. In this report, data for Mediterranean gull *Larus melanocephalus* are presented for the first time.

3.1 Red-throated diver *Gavia stellata*

Breeding numbers and breeding success (Figure 3.1.1, Table 3.1.1)

The timing of the breeding season in Shetland was earlier than in recent years due to good weather and reasonably high water levels in the spring. In the four areas monitored annually by the Shetland Ringing Group (Okill 2000a), there was a marked decline in the number of successful pairs, from 48 to 34, the lowest figure recorded since 1980 and consequently well below average for the period 1980 to 1999 (53.0, s.d. $\pm$ 7.95). The severe storm of 12 and 13 June proved destructive, with many pairs losing their eggs, especially those nesting on larger lochs and those on easterly shores. The timing of the storm was too late for many pairs to relay. The mean brood size at fledging in the study area was 1.31, slightly below the mean for the period 1979 to 1999 (1.36, s.e. $\pm$ 0.02).

Elsewhere in Shetland, mean breeding success was below the levels recorded in 1999 for all study areas except Foula. At this site, 12 pairs fledged four young, but productivity was still well below average. After the June storm three nests were found to be underwater. On Fetlar, 23 pairs were monitored but, after the very productive season in 1999, productivity was low at 0.57 chicks fledged per pair, though this was still above the long-term average (Smith & Luxford 2000). On Hermaness, productivity was consistent with recent years though well below the 1986-99 average, at 0.75 chicks fledged per pair (Rodger 2000).

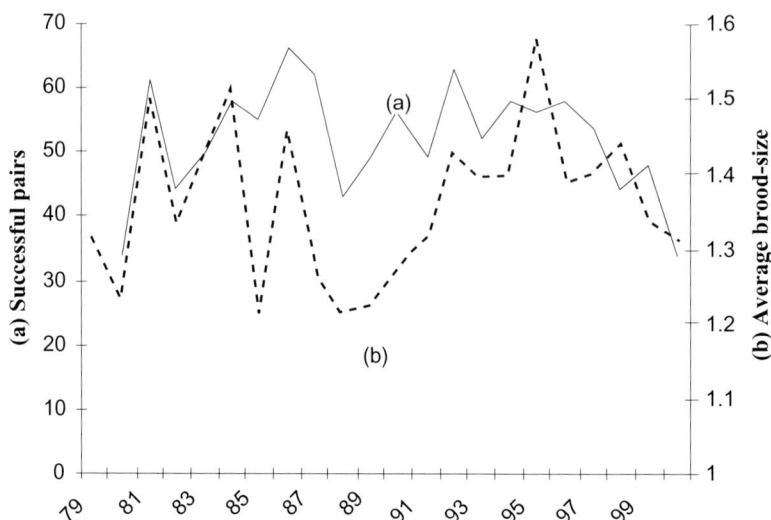

Figure 3.1.1 Annual variation in (a) numbers of 'successful' pairs (with chicks in mid-July) and (b) average brood-size near fledging at red-throated diver study areas in Shetland (parts of Unst, Eshaness, North Roe and Bressay), 1979-2000. Data are from Okill (2000a).

In Orkney, 80 monitored sites fledged an average of 0.59 chicks per site, above the long-term average of 0.52 (s.e. $\pm$ 0.03), but well below 1999 levels. On the Orkney mainland, 14 pairs fledged 0.86 chicks per pair, well above the 1986-99 mean of 0.53 (s.e. $\pm$ 0.07). On Hoy, 66 pairs raised 35 young.

The number of occupied sites on Hoy was up slightly on 1999 but productivity was down, even though the weather was better than normal during the incubation period. The severe gale in June did not appear to have had any effect (E.J. & S.J. Williams, pers. comm.). On Rousay, seven pairs attempted to breed, but only two chicks were seen subsequently and it is not known if they fledged.

Outside the Northern Isles, few data were available for 2000. On Rum, 12 pairs reared only five young, again well below the average since 1986. On the neighbouring island of Eigg, two pairs each hatched two young though all suffered predation, possibly by an otter, within three weeks (J. Chester, pers. comm.). However, it was another good year on Handa where four pairs fledged six young, well above the 1986-99 average.

Table 3.1.1 Red-throated diver breeding success, 1986-99, 1999 and 2000: figures are estimated number of chicks fledged per breeding pair or occupied site (Orkney). Note that numbers of pairs do not necessarily indicate total populations in study areas. Figures for Rousay in 2000 are not included in the Orkney sample total for that year.

	1986-99 mean		1999		2000	
	No. years	Fldg/pr (±s.e.)	Pairs	Fldg/pr	Pairs	Fldg/pr
Hermaness	14	1.01 (±0.10)	7	0.86	8	0.75
Fetlar	14	0.49 (±0.06)	22	0.91	23	0.57
Yell	12	0.62 (±0.09)	28	0.43	-	-
Foula	14	0.46 (±0.07)	13	0.23	12	0.33
Shetland sample total	12	0.60 (±0.05)	70	0.59	43	0.53
Hoy	11	0.55 (±0.03)	63	0.73	66	0.53
Rousay	10	0.25 (±0.12)	4	1.25	(7	0.00-0.29)
Mainland	11	0.53 (±0.07)	25	0.72	14	0.86
Orkney sample total	11	0.52 (±0.03)	92	0.75	80	0.59
Handa	13	1.23 (±0.12)	4	2.00	4	1.50
Eigg	14	0.98 (±0.15)	2	0.50	2	0.00
Rum	13	0.60 (±0.07)	8	0.37	12	0.42

3.2 Northern fulmar *Fulmarus glacialis*

Breeding numbers (Table 3.2.1, Figure 3.2.1)

Overall numbers of Northern fulmars breeding at monitored colonies increased across most regions between 1999 and 2000. In particular, there were overall increases at regularly monitored colonies in Shetland, on North Sea coasts of mainland Britain and in Wales, following some decline in the last few years (Figure 3.2.1). In Shetland, increases occurred at all four SOTEAG annual monitoring plots, though the only significant change was an 8.6% increase at Troswick Ness. However, upward population trends recorded in Shetland between 1986 and 1997 (Thompson *et al.* 1999, Figure 3.2.1) contrast with whole colony counts, which show huge declines in breeding numbers. For example, a whole colony count on Fair Isle found 20,424 apparently occupied sites (AOS), a huge decrease of 52.9% since the last count in 1996. A similar decline was also noted on Foula, where numbers had decreased by 54.8% to 21,106 AOS since the last count in 1987.

On Orkney mainland, triennial monitoring of numbers attending sample plots at five colonies revealed increases at four of the colonies. Significant increases occurred at Marwick Head (+19.3%, t=2.447, d.f.=9, P<0.05) and at Row Head (+23.9%, t=3.669, d.f.=11, P<0.01). A whole colony count of Costa Head totalled 2,827 AOS, indicative of an increase in the colony since a 1985 count of 2,548 individuals. On Papa Westray, a whole island count produced 294 AOS. An overall decline from 1999 levels on the west coast of Scotland masked considerable variation between colonies. Numbers on Canna increased by 14.8% to 443 AON after the low count recorded in 1999. On Handa, numbers were found to have declined by 17.9% to 3,550 AOS since the last complete survey in 1996. A decline of 33.5% was also noted along the south-east coast of Rum, from 433 AON in 1999 to 288 AON in 2000. On Colonsay, numbers increased by 7.1%, from 533 AOS in 1999 to 571 AOS in 2000.

In north-east Scotland, numbers at the Sands of Forvie increased by 22.4% from 1999, to 360 AOS, the highest figure recorded there. In south-east Scotland, numbers on the Isle of May increased by 17.6% from 1999 levels, to 367 AOS. A complete census of other islands in the Firth of Forth (Inchkeith, Inchgarvie, Inchcolm, Inchmickery, Craigleith, The Lamb and Fidra) also revealed an increase from 1999, by 10.9% to 1,241 AOS. Numbers at St. Abb's Head remained stable compared with 1999, at 274 AOS. In north-east England, numbers on the Farnes decreased slightly by 4.2%, from 264 AOS in 1999 to 253 AOS in 2000. In Wales, numbers at most colonies remained similar to those recorded in 1999, though numbers increased on Skomer by 18.9% to 691 AOS, the highest figure recorded at this site since 1995.

Table 3.2.1 Population changes at monitored Northern fulmar colonies, 1999-2000 (apparently occupied sites in late May or June). Counts with a reported inaccuracy of $> \pm 5\%$, and regional samples < 100 AOS, are excluded. Except where otherwise indicated, regional totals are derived from single complete counts of the colonies listed below.

	SW Scotland	NW Scotland	Shetland	NE Scotland	SE Scotland	NE England	Wales
1986-99 annual % change	0.0 n.s.	0.0 n.s.	+1.7***	-	+2.0**	+2.2*	+2.2**
1999	533	1,086	2,757	294	1,756	367	997
2000	571	1,028	2,977	360	1,950	393	1,095
1999-2000 % change	+7.1[a]	-5.3[b]	+8.0[c]	+22.4[d]	+11.0[e]	+7.1[f]	+9.8[g]

Colonies: [a] Colonsay (sample areas); [b] Canna, Eigg, Handa (plot counts), Rum (east coast); [c] Hermaness (productivity plot), Eshaness (plot counts), Burravoe (plot counts), Troswick Ness (plot counts), Sumburgh Head (plot counts), Fair Isle (productivity plots); [d] Sands of Forvie; [e] Isle of May, Inchkeith, Inchgarvie, Craigleith, Fidra, St. Abb's Head, Inchcolm, Inchmickery, The Lamb, Bass Rock; [f] Farne Islands, Huntcliff; [g] Stackpole Head plus Elegug Stacks & adjacent coastline, St. Margaret's Island, Caldey, Skomer, Skokholm, Bardsey, South Stack.

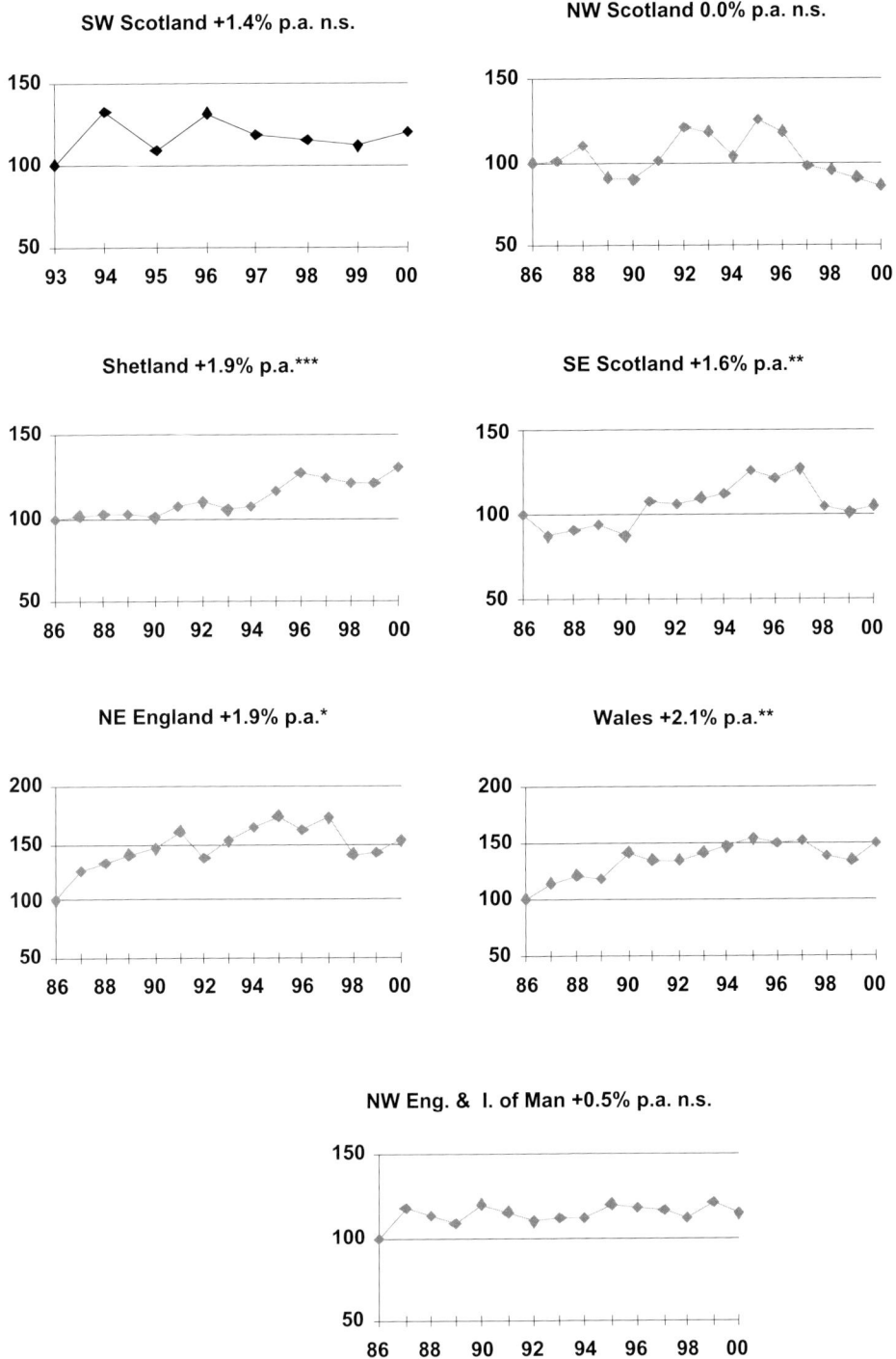

Figure 3.2.1 Regional population indices for breeding Northern fulmars, 1986-2000 (apparently occupied sites in June). Average annual rates of change were calculated by regression of natural log of index against year (see section 1.2.2. for details). Unless otherwise indicated, three or more colonies were counted in each year. Statistical significance of trends (t-test) indicated as: n.s. not significant, * P < 0.05, ** P < 0.01, ***P < 0.001.

Breeding success (Table 3.2.2)

In 2000, fulmars generally had a good breeding season, although there were variations between regions. Breeding success averaged 0.53 (s.e. ± 0.07) chicks fledged per AOS across 28 colonies, higher than the 1986-99 mean of 0.42 (s.e. ± 0.01).

Several colonies experienced poor breeding success. In north Scotland, the colony at North Sutor produced 0.34 chicks per AOS, the highest figure recorded here since 1994. Breeding success at sites in south-east Scotland was generally low, although higher than in 1999. At Tantallon, productivity reached 0.25 chicks per AOS compared with 0.19 in 1999, but was well below the 1987-99 mean of 0.41 (s.e. ± 0.04). Similarly, at St. Abb's Head, breeding success of 0.20 chicks per AOS was an improvement on 1999 (0.10), and on 1998 when the colony failed completely. On the Isle of May, breeding success was relatively poor with 0.37 chicks fledged per AOS, below the 1986-99 average of 0.43 (s.e. ± 0.02). In contrast, breeding success on the Farnes (north-east England) was the highest since 1994, with 0.59 chicks fledged per AOS, above the 1986-99 average of 0.53 (s.e. ± 0.03).

Table 3.2.2 Northern fulmar breeding success, 1999-2000: estimated number of chicks fledged per apparently occupied site at sample colonies (superscript n = number of colonies). Figures are based on regularly occupied sites or on the average numbers of occupied sites in June, and are presented as the means and standard errors of figures for individual colonies. Changes in breeding success are indicated for colonies where similar methods have been used in both years, none of these are statistically significant.

Region	1999 chicks fledged/site				2000 chicks fledged/site				1999-2000 change	
	AOS^n	Range	Mean	±s.e.	AOS^n	Range	Mean	±s.e.	$Mean^n$	±s.e.
SW Scotland[a]	23^1	-	0.83	-	17^1	-	0.53	-	-0.30^1	-
NW Scotland[b]	481^3	0.25-0.37	0.33	±0.04	478^3	0.24-0.44	0.37	±0.07	$+0.04^3$	±0.11
Shetland[c]	$3,041^8$	0.33-0.55	0.39	±0.02	$3,165^7$	0.30-0.68	0.46	±0.05	$+0.05^7$	±0.03
Orkney[d]	745^6	0.44-0.62	0.49	±0.03	875^6	0.29-0.73	0.44	±0.07	-0.05^6	±0.08
N Scotland[e]	112^2	0.11-0.12	0.11	±0.00	62^1	-	0.34	-	$+0.22^1$	-
SE Scotland[f]	289^3	0.11-0.47	0.25	±0.11	303^3	0.20-0.37	0.27	±0.05	$+0.02^3$	±0.06
NE England[g]	158^1	-	0.46	-	153^1	-	0.59	-	$+0.13^1$	-
SW England[h]	25^1	-	0.56	-	12^1	-	0.83	-	$+0.27^1$	-
Wales[i]	263^3	0.50-0.93	0.67	±0.13	308^3	0.33-0.91	0.57	±0.17	-0.09^3	±0.07
Isle of Man[j]	459^7	0.08-0.39	0.26	±0.04	25^1	-	0.40	-	-0.06^1	-
NE Ireland[k]	15^1	-	0.40	-	5^1	-	1.00	-	$+0.60^1$	-
Total	$5,611^{36}$	0.08-0.93	0.43	±0.06	$5,403^{28}$	0.20-0.91	0.53	±0.07	$+0.03^{28}$	±0.04

Colonies: [a] Ailsa Craig; [b] Canna, Handa, St Kilda; [c] Hermaness, Eshaness, Noss, Westerwick, Troswick Ness, Sumburgh Head, Fair Isle, Fetlar (1999 only); [d] Costa Head, Mull Head, Gultak, Rousay, North Ronaldsay, Papa Westray; [e] Easter Ross, Wilkhaven (1999 only); [f] Isle of May, Tantallon, St. Abb's Head; [g] Farne Islands; [h] West Bay-Burton Bradstock; [i] Skomer, Skokholm, Bardsey; [j] Traie Vane-Gob yn Ushtey (1999 only), Peel Hill (1999 only), Glen Maye, Bradda (1999 only), Marine Drive Douglas (1999 only), north of Peel (1999 only), Contrary Head-Traie Cronkan (1999 only); [k] Old Lighthouse Island.

Overall values for breeding success were similar between Shetland and Orkney in 2000, though compared to 1999, productivity had increased slightly in Shetland and decreased slightly in Orkney. On the west coast of Scotland, 0.48 chicks fledged per AOS on Canna, well above the 1986-99 average of 0.37 (s.e. ± 0.03). However, productivity on Handa (0.39 chicks per AOS), St Kilda (0.24) and Ailsa Craig (0.53) was below the long-term mean for each site. In Wales, overall productivity at three colonies monitored in 1999 and 2000 decreased by 0.09 chicks per AOS, though fortunes at these colonies were mixed. Breeding success at Bardsey was again exceptionally high, with 0.91 chicks per AOS (0.93 in 1999), and at Skokholm, success of 0.48 was just below average (0.50, s.e. ± 0.03). However, Skomer had its poorest year, with breeding success of 0.32 chicks per AOS being well below average (0.60, s.e. ± 0.04). On the Isle of Man, breeding success of 0.40

chicks per AOS was just above average (0.35, s.e. $\pm$ 0.04), although fewer nests were monitored than in previous years. In south-west England, productivity was 0.83 chicks per nest in a small colony at West Bay/Burton Bradstock. In Ireland, the only productivity data received was from Old Lighthouse Island, Copeland, where breeding success from five nests was estimated at 1.0 chick per nest.

3.3 Manx shearwater *Puffinus puffinus*

On Canna (north-west Scotland), there was no response to tape playback from *c.*240 burrows checked in the core area of the former Tarbert Road colony. In addition, none of the 40 study burrows previously used to monitor breeding success were occupied by breeding pairs in 2000. A further 50 burrows were checked at other traditional breeding sites, 30 at Bresgor and 20 at Am Beannan, with only one response. This species is probably now close to extinction on Canna (Swann 2000a). In an attempt to reduce predation, the National Trust for Scotland continued using rat boxes containing poisoned bait. On nearby Rum, the breeding season was slightly more successful than in the previous two years (Ramsay 2001). Occupancy was 71% in a sample of 120 monitored burrows and breeding success was 0.66 chicks fledged per occupied burrow, just below the 1994-99 average (0.68, s.e. $\pm$ 0.08). Rat activity is continuing to be monitored using chew sticks at this colony. The low numbers of chicks ringed (469 in 2000 versus 499 in 1999), despite greater effort searching for young, suggests there may still be a rat problem on the island.

Breeding success was again good on Skomer, with 0.61 chicks fledged per pair laying from 83 study burrows (Perrins 2000), above the 1991-99 average (0.56, s.e. $\pm$ 0.06). It was another productive breeding season on Bardsey, with 0.84 chicks fledged per pair from a sample of 50 occupied burrows. This is similar to the 1999 figure and above the 1996-99 average (0.80, s.e. $\pm$ 0.01). In north-east Ireland, survey work, using standard tape-playback methodology (Walsh *et al.* 1995), carried out on Lighthouse Island found 2,900 pairs. On nearby Big Copeland Island, a six-hour preliminary survey using the same methods recorded approximately 3,000 pairs (range 1,000 – 5,000). A more accurate figure cannot be derived at present due to uncertainty over the rather variable nesting density and low level of sampling (N. McKee, pers. comm.). The total number of chicks caught for ringing on Old Lighthouse Island was 448 in 2000 (1994-99 mean 544, s.d. 200) though effort was far lower than normal.

3.4 European storm-petrel *Hydrobates pelagicus*

There are inherent difficulties with accurate censuses of petrels, arising from their patchy distribution and nocturnal lives, the presence of non-breeders, and siting of nests deep within burrows, cavities or crevices in remote areas. Because of this, estimates for national breeding numbers of storm and Leach's petrels remain uncertain (Lloyd *et al.* 1991). However, more recently, a standardised method for repeatable surveys has been developed, involving the use of diurnal playback of the male's "purr" song (Gilbert *et al.* 1998a & b; Ratcliffe *et al.* 1998a). This method, first advocated by James & Robertson (1985), has recently been used for Seabird 2000 counts, and the results obtained from surveys on the Scalloway Islands, the Isles of Scilly and St Kilda, are discussed in this and the following species account. Other methods are also used to monitor populations on an annual basis. The count unit is the Apparently Occupied Site (AOS).

The usual sites on Mousa were checked on 10 September, and 49 chicks were ringed. This was higher than the 38 chicks found at the same time in 1999. There were a further eight nests with eggs or very small young and at least six other inaccessible chicks plus nine failed nests. These results were fairly typical of this colony, and indicate an apparently successful season (Okill 2000).

Using various count methods, around 200 apparently occupies sites (AOS) were recorded on Sanda, Kintyre on 21 June. This was the same as estimated in 1999 (Morton 2000).

A survey was carried out on the Scalloway Islands on 8-9 July using the diurnal playback method, and a minimum of 27 responses were obtained from three of the islands: Fore Holm, Sanda Stour and Little Havra (Okill & Fowler 2000). Response rates are known to vary considerably, depending on factors such as habitat and year. Assuming a quarter (95% LCL=0.23; UCL=0.27) of occupied nests responded to tape playback, established from a previous study on Mousa (Ratcliffe *et al.* 1998b), this gives an estimated total in the region of 108 (100-117) AOS. No responses were obtained from many other apparently suitable islands in the group.

A full census was carried out on the Isles of Scilly between 24 June and 13 July, also using the diurnal playback method. Eleven colonies were found, and a total of 469 responses obtained. A further 149 AOS were estimated from bootstrapping results from sample quadrats. By applying a correction factor of 2.86 (Ratcliffe *et al.* 1998), the total population was estimated as 1,475 (LCL=1,334; UCL=1,616) AOS (Heaney *et al.* in press). Comparisons with previous estimates for the islands were not possible as census methods differed.

3.5 Leach's storm-petrel *Oceanodroma leucorhoa*

See the preceding species account for the background to methodology and survey techniques.

A full census of the St Kilda archipelago (Hirta, Dun, Boreray and Soay) revealed a total of 42,707 AOS (LCL=31,840; UCL=58,328). Dun held 65% of the birds, followed by Boreray with 24%, Hirta with 6% and Soay with 5%. The response rate was 0.382 (95% CL = 0.338-0.422), ascertained from a day-time plot on Boreray (Newton *et al.* 2000). This is the first complete census to be carried out on St Kilda. In 1987, Tasker *et al.* (1988) estimated *c.*3,200-6,400 AOS on Boreray and established that birds were present on Hirta and Dun, although direct comparison with the 2000 count is not possible as census methods differed.

3.6 Northern gannet *Morus bassanus*

Breeding numbers (Table 3.6.1, Figure 3.6.1)

Counts carried out in 2000 indicate that the overall Northern gannet population in Britain is continuing to increase. Only the colony on Fair Isle was counted both in 1999 and in 2000. Also in Shetland, a whole colony count of Foula totalled 723 apparently occupied nests (AON), an increase of 20.5% since the last complete count in 1994.

Table 3.6.1 Population changes at an individual Northern gannet colony 1999-2000 (peak or single counts of apparently occupied nests in June-July).

	Fair Isle (Shetland)
1999	1,123
2000	1,162
% change 1999-2000	+3.5

The colony on Scar Rocks (south-west Scotland) was also found to have increased since the last comparable count in 1996; a boat-based survey found numbers had risen by 51.0% to 1,670 AON. In north-east Scotland, numbers at Troup Head remained largely unchanged since 1998, at 1,071 AOS. On Grassholm (Wales), a count from photographs taken in 1999 showed that the population had increased by 10.4% since 1994, to 30,688 apparently occupied sites (Murray 2000). A ground check in September 2000, to verify the breeding limits of the colony, confirmed the presence of a new sub-colony on the east side of the North Gut, which had been unused up to 1994.

Fair Isle   +10.1% p.a. ***

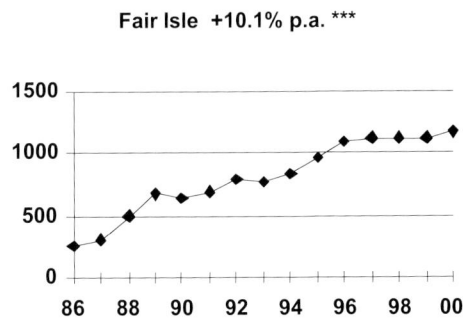

Figure 3.6.1 Northern gannet colony population trends for Fair Isle, 1986-2000. Figures are counts of AON. Trend is average annual rate of change. Significance of trend indicated as: *** P<0.001. Further details of calculation of trends are given in section 1.2.2.

Breeding success (Table 3.6.2)

The mean breeding success across five colonies monitored in 2000 was 0.66 chicks fledged per occupied nest, just below the 1986-99 mean of 0.69 (s.e. $\pm$ 0.03, based on between three and six colonies annually). At Hermaness, breeding success was the lowest on record, possibly as a result of the June storm, which also affected breeding success on Fair Isle. However, the below average productivity at these sites was not mirrored on Noss, which is well sheltered from the south-west and probably was protected from the worst of the storm. On Ailsa Craig, breeding success was much improved after the poor year of 1999.

Table 3.6.2 Northern gannet breeding success, 1986-99, 1999 and 2000: estimated number of chicks fledged per occupied nest. In 1999 and 2000, with the exception of Fair Isle, productivity is shown as the mean and standard error of figures from sample plots (superscript n = number of plots). The 1999 and 2000 figures for Fair Isle are for all nests totalled across sample plots.

Colony	1986-99 fledged /nest			1999 fledged/nest			2000 fledged/nest		
	Years	Mean	$\pm$ s.e.	AON^n	Mean	$\pm$ s.e.	AON^n	Mean	$\pm$ s.e.
Ailsa Craig (SW Scotland)	9	0.68	$\pm$0.02	110^1	0.61	-	215^2	0.71	$\pm$0.06
Hermaness (Shetland)	11	0.66	$\pm$0.02	713^3	0.69	$\pm$0.02	699^3	0.57	$\pm$0.02
Noss (Shetland)	14	0.68	$\pm$0.01	454^4	0.74	$\pm$0.02	464^4	0.73	$\pm$0.02
Fair Isle (Shetland)	14	0.69	$\pm$0.03	161^1	0.59	-	195^1	0.59	-
Troup Head (NE Scotland)	5	0.54	$\pm$0.04	-	-	-	$1,071^1$	$\leq$0.70	-
All colonies	-	0.69	$\pm$0.03	1,438	0.66	$\pm$0.04	2,644	0.66	$\pm$0.03

3.7 Great cormorant *Phalacrocorax carbo*

Breeding numbers (Table 3.7.1, Figure 3.7.1)

Most of the data summarised here were compiled from various sources by Dr. R.M. Sellers, organiser of the Cormorant Breeding Colony Survey (Sellers 2001). It should be noted that counts of breeding pairs of cormorants can be difficult to interpret, particularly where regional coverage is incomplete; birds may move between colonies and variable proportions of adults breed each year.

Between 1999 and 2000, overall numbers at colonies in the north and east of Britain generally declined, while those in the south and west increased. An exception to this geographical split occurred in south-east Scotland, where numbers increased, and at some individual colonies in Wales and the Isle of Man, which decreased.

In south-west Scotland, the colony at Port O'Warren increased by 31.2% to 126 AON, and numbers also increased at Currarie-Portandea by 20.7% to 128 apparently occupied nests (AON). Both of these colonies had suffered declines between 1998 and 1999, of 29% and 26% respectively. In south-east Scotland, a complete count of four colonies in the Firth of Forth (Inchkeith, Carr Craig, Craigleith and The Lamb) found 440 AON, an increase of 17.3% on 1999; all had increased since 1999 except The Lamb where numbers remained stable. In north-west England and the Isle of Man, there was a 3.4% increase in numbers at colonies counted in both 1999 and 2000. At St. Bees Head (31 AON) and Wills Strand (Isle of Man) (26 AON) numbers were the highest recorded since 1986. However, elsewhere on the Isle of Man, a slight decrease occurred at Maughold Head with 81 AON recorded (84 AON in 1999) and no nests were found at Gob ny Skeddan (22 AON in 1999).

Table 3.7.1 Population changes at monitored great cormorant colonies, 1999-2000 (apparently occupied nests in May-June). Regional samples of fewer than 50 AON or of only one colony are excluded. Trends for 1986-99 are average annual rates of change shown by sample populations. Significance of trends indicated as: n.s. not significant, * P<0.05, ** P<0.01, *** P<0.001). Further details of calculation of trends are given in section 1.2.2.

	SW Scotland	Shetland	N Scotland	SE Scotland	NE England
1986-99 annual % change	+1.4 n.s.	-5.4***	-3.0 n.s.	0.0 n.s.	0.0 n.s.
1999	348	98	315	375	197
2000	419	87	295	440	181
1999-2000 % change	+20.4[a]	-11.2[b]	-6.35[c]	+17.3[d]	-8.1[e]

	Inland England	SW England	NW England & Isle of Man	Wales	NE Ireland
1986-99 annual % change	+17.5***	-1.5 n.s.	+2.9*	+0.9 n.s.	+5.9***
1999	142	124	145	631	271
2000	166	132	150	604	278
1999-2000 % change	+16.9[f]	+6.5[g]	+3.4[h]	-4.3[i]	+2.6[j]

Colonies: [a] Port O' Warren, Currarie-Portandea, Balkenna, Sanda, Eilean na Cille, Corr Eilean, Eilean Dubh, Eilean Buidhe, Eilean Buidhe (Black Harbour); [b] Clett Stacks, Heads of Grocken; [c] Stack of Ulbster, Stacks of Occumster, Ceann Leathad, Neuk Mhor, Ord Point, North Sutor, Dun Glas; [d] Carr Craig, The Lamb, Long Craig & Inchkeith, Craigleith; [e] Farne Islands, Boulby Cliff; [f] Dungeness (Kent), Aldermaston, Rutland; [g] Ballard Cliff, Gad Cliff, Carswell Cove; [h] St. Bee's Head, Wills Strand, Pistol Castle, Maughold Head; [i] Skomer, St. Margaret's Island, Yns Gwylan, Gwynedd A, Rhoscolyn Beacon, Great Orme, Little Orme; [j] Bird Island, Black Rock.

After the 31% decline reported in 1999, numbers in south-west England improved slightly, increasing by 6.5% at regularly monitored colonies. An increase of 16.9 % was recorded at a limited sample of inland colonies in England, which were counted in May or June in both 1999 and 2000 (Table 3.7.1). However, the overall trend is unclear as a late April count of the largest colony at Abberton Reservoir found only 370 AON, down from 423 in 1999.

In Wales, there was considerable variation between colonies in changes in numbers between 1999 and 2000. Increases occurred at Little Orme (6.6% to 183 AON) and at Ynys Gwylan (17.8% to 53 AON). In addition, two previously small colonies increased substantially between 1999 and 2000.

Numbers increased at Great Orme from 13 to 46 AON, and at Rhoscolyn Beacon from 9 to 31 AON. On St. Margaret's Island, numbers fell for the second successive year to a new low of 149 AON, a decline of 13.4%. After increasing between 1998 and 1999, the colony "A" in Gwynedd declined by 41.0%, from 210 AON to 124 AON. In Ireland, the colony in Strangford Lough (Co. Down) increased slightly from 271 AON to 278 AON, the highest figure recorded since 1986.

In Shetland, numbers at Clett Stacks, which in 1999 held nearly 50% of the islands' population, declined from 94 AON to 83 AON, continuing the long-term decline at this site. Elsewhere, Ramna Stacks was deserted for the third consecutive year (Okill 2000b). In Orkney, a count in late August on Boray Holm, the largest colony, revealed a decline from 169 AON in 1999 to 120 AON in 2000.

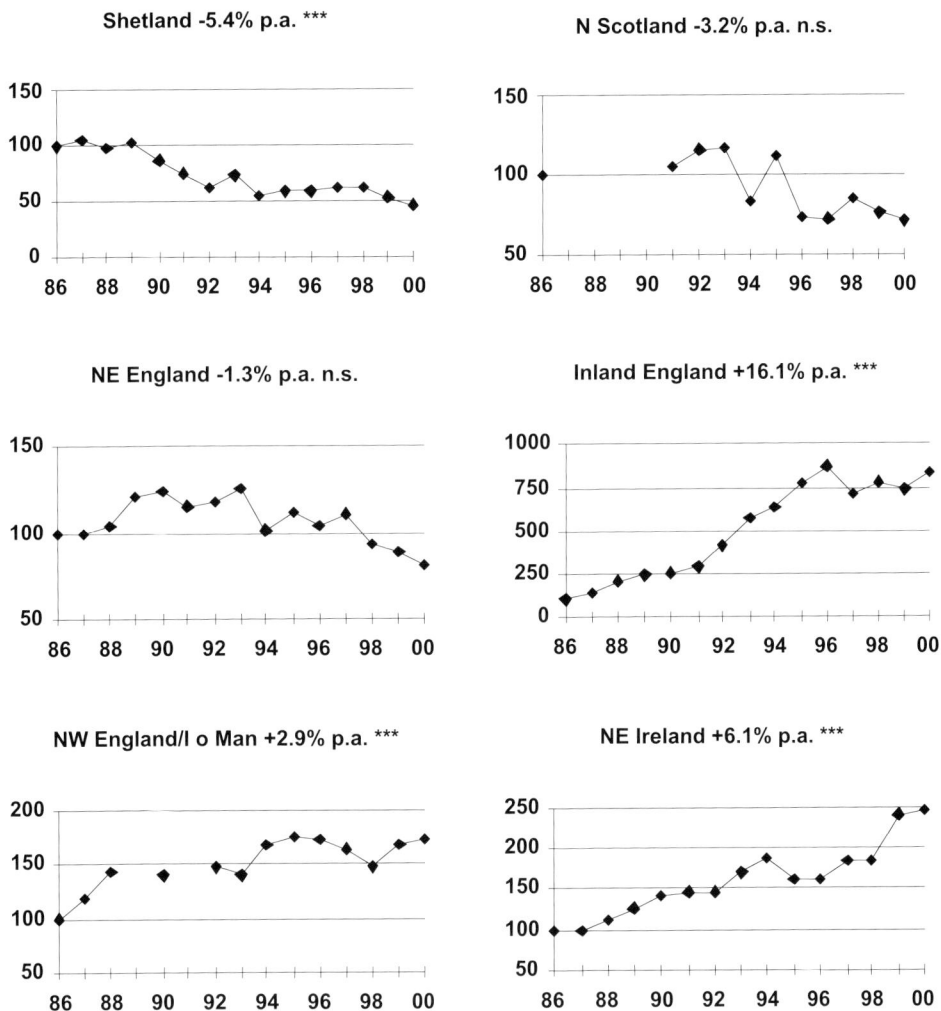

Figure 3.7.1 Regional population indices for breeding great cormorant, 1986-2000 (apparently occupied nests). Trends are average annual rates of change shown by sample populations. Significance of trends indicated as: ** P<0.01, *** P < 0.001. Further details of calculation of trends are given in section 1.2.2.

In northern Scotland, numbers in Caithness fell again, from 114 AON in 1999 to only 109 in 2000. The colony at North Sutor declined for the second successive year to 186 AON, a decrease of 7.5% from 1999. In north-east England, breeding numbers on the Farnes fell to 146 AON, the lowest recorded since 1986 and, though numbers have been variable, there is evidence of a long term decline at this site, and across the region as a whole, since 1989.

Breeding success

Few data were received in 2000. However, breeding success appeared to be close to the norm for this species in Britain, with broods of between two and three chicks fledged per successful nest. In Shetland, it was noted as being an exceptionally early breeding season resulting in few chicks being ringed due to their large size and the need to avoid undue disturbance at the time of colony visits. Mean brood size at Ceann Leathad in Caithness was 2.21 chicks, an improvement after the poor year in 1999 (1.59) but still below the 1993 to 1999 average for this site (2.33, s.e. ± 0.16). At North Sutor (Easter Ross), breeding success in a sample of 96 nests was 2.45 chicks per nest, well above the 1991-99 mean for this colony (1.97, s.e. ± 0.18). In western Scotland, a minimum of 314 young fledged from 172 nests at six colonies, equivalent to a minimum of 1.83 per pair (Craik 2000). In Wales, the colony on Ynysoedd Gwylan fledged an average of 1.98 chicks per pair. On the Isle of Man, the colony at Wills Strand produced 2.38 chicks per pair from 21 successful nests.

3.8 European shag *Phalacrocorax aristotelis*

Breeding numbers (Table 3.8.1, Figure 3.8.1)

Between 1999 and 2000, populations of European shags were found to have increased in the majority of regions (Table 3.8.1). These increases were particularly striking along North Sea coasts where there had been marked declines in the previous year. This immediate recovery in populations indicates that low attendance, rather than over-winter adult mortality, caused the reductions in numbers of nests in 1999. However, populations in both south-east Scotland and north-east England have yet to recover from the crash of the early 1990s.

Table 3.8.1 Population changes at monitored European shag colonies, 1999-2000 (apparently occupied nests in May-June). Counts with a reported inaccuracy of $> \pm 5\%$, and regional samples < 100 AON, are excluded. Trends for 1986-99 are average annual rates of change shown by sample populations. Significance of trends indicated as: n.s. not significant, ** P<0.01, *** P<0.001). Further details of calculation of trends are given in section 1.2.2.

	SW Scotland	NW Scotland	Shetland	N Scotland	SE Scotland	NE England	Wales
% annual change	1994-99 +3.9 n.s.	1987-99 -4.7**	1986-99 -5.4***	-	1994-99 +0.3 n.s.	1994-99 +2.9 n.s.	-
1999	1080	933	335	266	783	940	219
2000	1057	1063	488	292	1283	1310	239
1999-2000% change	-2.1[a]	+13.9[b]	+45.7[c]	+9.8[d]	+63.9[e]	+39.4[f]	+9.1[g]

Colonies: [a] Colonsay (sample plots), Sanda Island, Lunga, Carraig an Daimh, Eilean Buidhe, Ruadh Sgeir, Eilean na Cille, Eileanan Glasa; [b] Eigg, Canna, Rum (east coast), An Glas Eilean, Handa (plot), Eilean Balnagowan; [c] Fair Isle (plots), Noss, Sumburgh Head; [d] North Sutor; [e] Isle of May, Inchkeith, Fidra, Inchmickery, Inchcolm, Haystack, Carr Craig, Craigleith, The Lamb, Bass Rock, St. Abb's Head; [f] Farne Islands; [g] Ynys Gwylan Fawr, Bardsey, St. Margaret's Island, Caldey Island, Skomer, Middleholm, Stackpole Head & nearby coast, Elegug Stacks, Little Orme.

In south-east Scotland, the number of apparently occupied nests (AON) on the Isle of May increased by 108.9% to 541 AON, a reversal of the decline of 58% recorded between 1998 and 1999, though numbers are still down on the 1998 figure (621 AON). There was also an increase in numbers at eight islands in the Firth of Forth, up 46.2%, from 329 AON in 1999 to 481 AON in 2000. Numbers also increased at St. Abb's Head, by 41.2% to 233 AON. In north-east England, numbers on the Farnes increased after two years of declines. A count of 1,310 AON was up 39.4% on 1999 and was the highest figure recorded at the site since 1993. In Shetland, numbers also recovered from 1999, when gales forced many birds to abandon nesting attempts (Upton *et al.* 2000). Following a prolonged decline, which culminated in the low reached in 1993, there has been a gradual increase in numbers in Shetland (Heubeck 2000). The only mainland colony counted in 1999 and 2000 was at Sumburgh

Head, where numbers increased by 36.2% to 252 AON. On Noss, numbers also increased between 1999 and 2000, by 50% to 81 AON. On Fair Isle, numbers at five monitoring plots increased by 61.5% between 1999 and 2000, reversing a long-term decline which reached a low in 1999 (Shaw *et al.* 2000). On Foula, a whole colony count recorded 2,277 AON, a decline of only 5.0% since the last complete count in 1987.

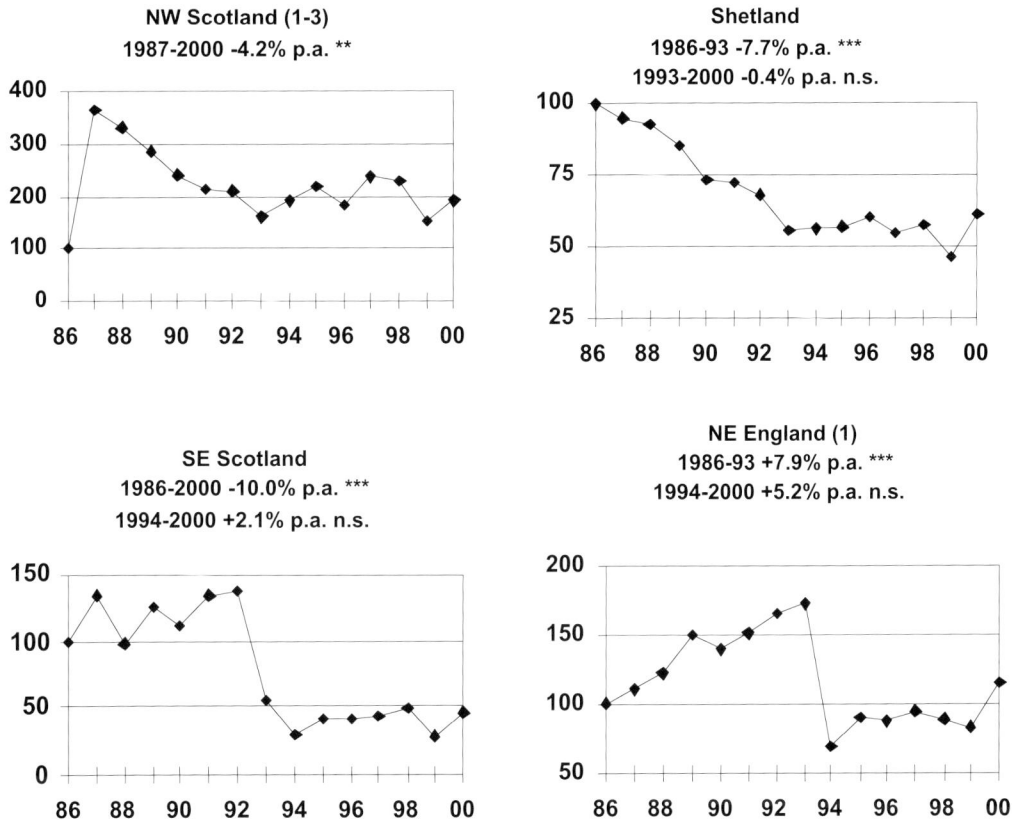

Figure 3.8.1 Population indices for breeding European shags, 1986-2000 (apparently occupied nests in late May or June). Three or more colonies are counted in each region in each year unless otherwise indicated. Trends for 1986-2000 are average annual rates of change shown by sample populations for the periods indicated, but note that overall trends may mask shorter term population fluctuations. Significance of trends (t-test) indicated as: n.s. not significant, ** P<0.01, *** P<0.001. Further details of calculation of trends are given in section 1.2.2.

At North Sutor in northern Scotland, numbers increased for the fourth successive year to 292 AON, an increase of 9.8% from 1999. Numbers at monitored colonies in north-west Scotland increased overall in 2000 by 13.9%. After the decline recorded between 1998 and 1999, numbers on Canna increased to 838 AON from 742 AON. On Handa, there was little change in numbers between 1999 (105 AON) and 2000 (109 AON). There was little change in overall numbers at monitored colonies in south-west Scotland, though numbers on Lunga fell by 11.9% to 260 AON. In Wales, there was a slight overall increase at colonies monitored in 1999 and 2000 (Table 3.8.1). Numbers at Ynys Gwylan, the largest colony monitored, were little changed at 133 AON.

Breeding Success (Table 3.8.2)

Across ten colonies where productivity was assessed by monitoring sample nests throughout the breeding season, an average of 1.34 chicks fledged per active nest in 2000, above the 1986-99 mean of 1.30 (s.e. ± 0.06) averaged over between three and 20 colonies annually. This was higher than the 1999 average of 1.06 chicks fledged per pair, and across the ten colonies monitored in both years, breeding success increased by an average of 0.23 chicks per pair.

The most marked improvement in breeding success was in south-east Scotland. Breeding success at St. Abb's Head was 1.56 chicks fledged per pair, higher than the 1990-99 mean of 1.23 (s.e $\pm$ 0.15) and the highest since 1996. On the Isle of May, breeding success was an improvement on 1999, with 1.48 chicks fledged per pair overall, the highest figure recorded and hence well above the 1986-99 average (0.78, s.e. $\pm$ 0.08) (Wilson 2000). However, in north-east England, breeding success on the Farnes was 0.65 chicks per pair, far lower than the long-term mean of 1.07 (s.e. $\pm$ 0.12).

Table 3.8.2 European shag breeding success, 1999-2000: estimated number of chicks fledged per occupied nest at sample colonies (superscript n = number of colonies). Figures are based on nests where eggs or apparent incubation were recorded, and are presented as the mean and standard error of figures for individual colonies. Only colonies where ten or more nests were monitored are included. The figures used for some colonies in both years in SW Scotland as well as for An Glas Eilean in NW Scotland are based on just one or a few visits and are hence approximate, those for other colonies and regions are based on regular checks of sample nests. Changes in breeding success are indicated for colonies studied in both years, none of these are statistically significant.

Regions	1999 chicks fledged/nest				2000 chicks fledged/nest				1999-2000 change	
	Nests[n]	Range	Mean	$\pm$s.e.	Nests[n]	Range	Mean	$\pm$s.e.	Mean[n]	$\pm$s.e.
SW Scotland[a]	300[6]	0.37-1.63	$\geq$1.19	$\pm$0.24	285[6]	0.91-2.15	$\geq$1.48	$\pm$0.24	+0.23	$\pm$0.28
NW Scotland[b]	74[2]	$\leq$0.35-0.91	$\leq$0.63	$\pm$0.28	82[2]	0.80-0.91	$\geq$0.86	$\pm$0.06	+0.23[2]	$\pm$0.32
Shetland[c]	288[3]	1.01-1.13	$\geq$1.08	$\pm$0.04	304[3]	0.46-1.84	1.04	$\pm$0.41	-0.04[3]	$\pm$0.40
N Scotland[d]	78[1]	-	1.36	-	74[1]	-	1.66	-	+0.30[1]	-
SE Scotland[e]	103[2]	0.33-0.93	0.63	$\pm$0.30	198[2]	1.53-1.56	1.54	$\pm$0.02	+0.91[2]	$\pm$0.28
NE England[f]	369[1]	-	0.62	-	137[1]	-	0.65	-	+0.03[1]	-
Wales[g]	195[3]	1.80-2.00	$\leq$1.93	$\pm$0.07	177[2]	1.78-2.27	2.03	$\pm$0.24	+0.12[2]	$\pm$0.14
Total	1,407[18]	0.33-2.00	1.15	$\pm$0.13	1,257[17]	0.46-2.15	1.36	$\pm$0.14	+0.27[14]	$\pm$0.14
Detailed only	1,274[14]	0.33-2.00	1.06	+0.14	939[10]	0.80-2.27	1.34	0.19	0.22[10]	$\pm$0.17

Colonies: [a] Ruadh Sgeir, Eilean Buidhe, Eilean Dubh (2000 only), Eilean na Cille, Eileanan Glasa, Craro (2000 only), Corr Eilean (1999 only); [b] Canna, An Glas Eilean; [c] Sumburgh Head, Fair Isle, Foula; [d] North Sutor; [e] Isle of May, St. Abb's Head; [f] Farne Islands; [g] Bardsey, Ynys Gwylan, Middleholm (1999 only).

At North Sutor in northern Scotland, breeding success was higher than average at 1.66 chicks per pair (mean 1992-99, 1.50, s.e. $\pm$ 0.13). In Shetland, breeding success at Sumburgh Head was 0.89 chicks per pair, the lowest recorded figure since 1990, largely due to south-westerly gales and heavy seas which washed out nests or killed chicks on four occasions. Had it not been for the gales, breeding success at Sumburgh Head would probably have been high, as three more sheltered plots on the east side of the headland achieved success ranging between 1.70-1.80 chicks per pair (Heubeck 2000). In contrast to 1999, productivity at Fair Isle was the highest recorded since 1986, at 1.84 chicks per pair, well above the 1986-99 mean of 1.39 (s.e. $\pm$ 0.06). The plot used for studying breeding productivity lies on the east side of the isle, so was sheltered from the south-westerly gales in June. European shags nesting on the west side of Fair Isle were estimated to have suffered losses of 40-50%.

In western Scotland, six colonies containing 280 nests monitored by Clive Craik fledged a minimum of 1.47 chicks per AON. Breeding success on Canna was the lowest recorded in the period since 1986 at 0.80 chicks per pair (mean 1.39, s.e. $\pm$ 0.09). Many nests on the outer edge of the Garrisdale sub-colony were empty, whilst those in the middle held chicks, suggesting predation as a contributory factor to the low breeding success (Swann 2000a). Breeding success continued to be high in Wales, and averaged 2.03 chicks per AON across two monitored colonies.

3.9 Arctic skua *Stercorarius parasiticus*

Breeding numbers (Table 3.9.1)

Overall numbers at 13 sites in Shetland fell for the third successive year, from 308 to 302 apparently occupied territories (AOT). This was despite numbers at the largest of these colonies, on Foula, increasing for the first time in some years. Adult survival on Foula was again high (Furness 2000). On Fair Isle, the count was the lowest recorded since 1987, at 65 AOT, (Shaw *et al.* 2000). At the eleven other regularly monitored sites in Shetland, overall numbers fell for the first time since 1997, with the most notable decline occurring on Fetlar, from 20 (Croft & Marks 1999), to 17 AOT (Smith & Luxford 2000).

In Orkney, overall numbers in the five traditional study plots remained stable. There was variation between sites, with increases occurring at Lushan, Mainland, from 29 to 34 AOT, and at Gallo Hill, Westray, from 24 to 28 AOT. However, in the study plot at North Hill, Papa Westray, numbers fell from 35 to 26 AOT (J. Williams pers. comm.). This downward trend was also evident on the North Hill reserve as a whole, and a complete count found just 67 AOT (Meek 2000), less than half 1990-99 levels. A whole island census of Hoy revealed 70 AOT, 63% below the 190 pairs counted within Hoy SSSI in 1989. Elsewhere, there were single AOTs on Auskerry and North Ronaldsay.

Numbers continued to increase on Handa, north-west Scotland, where a complete census found 40 AOT. Following a rat eradication programme in 1997 there were no sightings of brown rat in 2000 (Stoneman 2000).

Table 3.9.1 Population changes at monitored Arctic skua colonies, 1998-2000 (apparently occupied territories). Superscript = number of colonies counted in both years.

	Foula	Fair Isle	Other Shetland	Total Shetland	Orkney	Handa
1998	114	67	132	313	127	32
1999	106	69	133	308	123	35
2000	107	65	130	302	123	40
1999-2000 % change	+0.9	-5.8	-2.2[11]	-1.9[13]	0.0[5]	+14.3

Breeding success (Table 3.9.2)

The end of the ten-year monitoring project in Shetland and Orkney in 1999 meant that many fewer productivity data were available in 2000.

Overall productivity of five sites in Shetland (including Foula) was moderate, with *c.*120 chicks fledging from 210 AOT. Birds on Fair Isle had a below average season, with 24 young fledging from 65 AOT; great skuas were responsible for the deaths of at least 20 chicks. On Noss, only 0.22 chicks fledged per AOT, which, with the exception of 1998, was the lowest since 1989-90. Failure was generally attributed to a lack of available sandeels during the last two weeks of June and the first week of July, but there was also some great skua predation of chicks and adults (Upton & Maher 2000). At Hermaness, six young fledged from 12 AOT, a vast improvement on 1998-99 levels, but below the 1990-99 mean (0.67, s.e. ± 0.12). However, post-fledging predation by great skuas may have accounted for the loss of five of these fledglings (Rodger 2000). Breeding success on Foula was higher than 1999 levels, with about 0.8 young fledged per pair. As well as the usual great skua predation, the storm of 12/13 June resulted in the loss of many eggs and chicks (Furness 2000). Elsewhere in Shetland, success was poor on Papa Stour with most pairs apparently having failed, but at least 14 chicks fledged from South Bressay (Okill 2000b).

Breeding success at North Hill, Papa Westray was much lower than in 1999, with just 27 chicks fledging from 67 AOT. In addition, three pairs at Trumland, Rousay, completely failed, and one pair on North Ronaldsay fledged two young.

Table 3.9.2 Arctic skua breeding success in 1999 and 2000: number of chicks fledged per apparently occupied territory (AOT). Note that the same colonies have not necessarily been monitored in each region each year and that the numbers of AOT's given here are sample sizes (and do not necessarily indicate population changes between years). Superscript indicates number of colonies. (- indicates that no data were available). Note that data from Foula are now included.

Colony	1999		2000	
	AOT	overall numbers fledged per AOT	AOT	overall numbers fledged per AOT
Shetland				
Unst	35[2]	0.26	12[1]	0.50
Fetlar	20	0.20	17	0.18
Yell	23[2]	0.13	-	-
Noss	10	0.30	9	0.22
Mousa	18	0.33	-	-
Mainland	27[4]	0.85	-	-
Fair Isle	69	0.64	65	0.37
Foula	106	*c.*0.60	107	*c.*0.80
Shetland total	202 [12]	0.46	210[5]	0.57
Orkney				
Papa Westray	35[1]	1.49	67[1]	0.40
Westray	24[1]	0.71	-	-
Rousay	31[1]	0.39	3[1]	0.00
Mainland	29[1]	0.72	-	-
Hoy	4[1]	0.00	-	-
N Ronaldsay	-	-	1[1]	2.00
Orkney total	123[5]	0.83	71[3]	0.41

3.10 Great skua *Stercorarius skua*

Breeding numbers (Table 3.10.1)

With the end of the ten-year monitoring project, comparable data were available from only six sites in Shetland in 2000. On Fair Isle, numbers increased slightly, to 135 AOT (Shaw *et al.* 2000), and a slight increase in numbers was also recorded at five further sites. However, as the Noss count from 1999 was thought to be an underestimate, there was probably no real increase in total numbers in 2000. At three sites on Fetlar, overall numbers fell by eight AOT, to 52 (Smith & Luxford 2000), the lowest level since 1994. In the traditional study plot at Hermaness, Unst, there were 41 AOT (30 in 1998) (Rodger 2000). On Foula, birds had a very late season, with adult survival again high (Furness 2000).

In Orkney, overall numbers at six study plots fell by 10.5%, to 94 AOT, the lowest level since monitoring began in 1991. This was largely attributable to a decline at Lyrawa Hill, Hoy, from 30 to 21 AOT (J Williams pers. comm.). In addition, a decrease in numbers was also reported from North Hill, Papa Westray, where nine AOT were counted, down from 11 AOT in 1999 (Meek 2000).

A complete census of Handa revealed 195 AOT, 27 more than in 1999 (Stoneman 2000). One pair was also reported as holding territory on Canna, a new colonisation for the island (Swann 2000a).

Table 3.10.1 Population changes at monitored great skua colonies, 1998-2000 (apparently occupied territories). * The Fair Isle count in 1998 and Noss count in 1999 are thought to be underestimates. Superscript = number of colonies counted in both years.

	Fair Isle	Other Shetland	Total Shetland	Orkney	Handa
1998	79*	119	198	133	165
1999	132	107*	239	105	168
2000	135	114	249	94	195
1999-2000 % change	+2.3	$+6.5^{5}$	$+4.2^{6}$	-10.5^{6}	+16.1

Breeding success (Table 3.10.2)

Overall breeding success at six sites in Shetland was similar to 1999 levels for the same sites. Birds had a very successful season on Fetlar, with 61 young fledged from 52 pairs. At Hermaness, Unst, 35 chicks fledged from 41 AOT, almost equal to the 1990-99 mean of 0.87 (s.e. ± 0.08) (Rodger 2000). On Noss, 31 chicks fledged from 57 AOT. About 40% of chicks were lost to cannibalism, a much higher rate than recorded in 1998-99; as well as the lack of available alternative food, there was a pair in the study area specialising in chick predation. However, stomach flushing of a random sample of chicks showed that herring predominated in the diet, with no evidence of bird predation (Upton & Maher 2000). Birds had another successful season on Fair Isle, with up to 100 chicks fledging from 135 AOT (Shaw *et al.* 2000). On Foula, breeding success only reached 0.8 chicks fledged per nest. The storm of 12/13 June may have washed out some nests, but substantial numbers of chicks were killed by adults from the start of July. Chick regurgitates showed a near complete lack of sandeels from this time with whitefish predominating in the diet (Furness 2000).

Productivity data were only available for twelve pairs at three sites in Orkney. At North Hill, Papa Westray, nine AOT fledged seven young (Meek 2000), slightly above average for this site. Elsewhere, two pairs fledged two chicks at Trumland, Rousay, and one pair failed at Hobbister, Mainland.

Table 3.10.2 Great skua breeding success in 1999 and 2000: number of chicks fledged per apparently occupied territory (AOT). Note that the same colonies have not necessarily been monitored in each region each year and that the numbers of AOT given here are sample sizes (and do not necessarily indicate population changes between years). Superscript indicates number of colonies (- indicates that no data were available).

Colony	1999		2000	
	AOT	overall numbers fledged per AOT	AOT	overall numbers fledged per AOT
Shetland				
Unst	94	1.10	41	0.85
Fetlar	60^3	0.48	52	1.17
Mainland	46^2	0.39	-	-
Yell	32^2	0.31	-	-
Mousa	18	0.56	-	-
Noss	43	0.70	57	0.54
Fair Isle	132	0.77	135	0.74
Shetland total	425	0.71	285	0.80
Orkney				
NW Hoy	35	0.49	-	-
S Hoy	27	0.33	-	-
E Hoy	30	0.53	-	-
Westray	5	0.80	-	-
Mainland	5	0.40	1	0.00
Rousay	3	0.67	2	1.00
Papa Westray	11	0.82	9	0.78
Orkney total	116	0.51	12	0.75

3.11 Mediterranean gull *Larus melanocephalus*

Breeding numbers and breeding success

This is the first year that Mediterranean gull features in the report. An extreme rarity in Britain as recently as the 1930s, the numbers seen along our shores have increased substantially in recent decades. Colonies around the Black Sea increased in size, from an estimated 93,500 pairs in 1961 to a minimum of 330,000 pairs in 1982 (Cramp & Simmons 1983; Siokhin *et al.* 1988), and with this increase has come a range expansion westwards. A small central European breeding population established itself in Hungary in the late 1950's, since when breeding has occurred in most west European countries. Breeding in Britain was first recorded in 1968, but it was not until 1979 that this became an annual event. Since then the number of nesting pairs has increased, a trend mirrored in other countries in central and Western Europe (Donald & Bekhuis 1993). Now the breeding population in the United Kingdom numbers almost 70 pairs (Ogilvie *et al.* 2000).

At present, few data are received though it is hoped that, by including the species in the annual report more will be forthcoming in future years. In 2000, data were received from six sites in east and south-east England. In Hampshire, the main site held 38 pairs that fledged 41 young. Data from a second site indicated that up to five pairs were present, of which one pair is thought to have been successful fledging one young. In Essex, two or three pairs nested at one site without success. Data were received from three sites in Kent. At two sites close to each other, 23 pairs nested but no information was available on productivity. No pairs nested at the third site in 2000.

3.12 Black-headed gull *Larus ridibundus*

Breeding numbers and breeding success (Table 3.12.1)

Black-headed gulls are highly mobile between breeding sites; hence, the changes in numbers at sample colonies shown in Table 3.12.1 are not necessarily representative of broader regional trends.

Table 3.12.1 Population changes at monitored black-headed gull colonies, 1999-2000 (breeding pairs, apparently incubating adults or apparently occupied nests in May-June).

	W Scotland	SE England	SW England	NE Ireland
1999	243	9,358	231	3,851
2000	178	9,380	199	2,056
1999-2000 % change	-26.7[a]	+0.2[b]	-13.9[c]	-46.6[d]

Colonies: [a] Eilean Inshaig, Sgeir na Caillich, Dubh Sgeir, Eilean Fada, Airds Islet, Torinturk, Duncuan, Eilean Choinneich; [b] Rye Harbour, North Solent NNR, Flanders Mare, Dungeness; [c] Brownsea Island; [d] Strangford Lough, Cockle Island.

In western Scotland, overall numbers at monitored colonies declined by 27%. At nine sites in Clive Craik's study area, breeding success from 188 pairs was 1.29 chicks per pair, far higher than that recorded in recent years (0.34 in 1999, 0.24 in 1998, 0.47 in 1997, 0.42 in 1996). Almost all (99%) of the young were at four sites where mink *Mustela vison* are controlled annually, 90% of the young were at one site where black-headed gulls disappeared after four successive years of mink predation caused total failure, but which has now been restored to its pre mink numbers (Craik 2000).

In Shetland, numbers on Fetlar decreased from 102 pairs in 1999 to only nine pairs in 2000, all of which suffered predation at the egg stage (Smith & Luxford 2000). Once again, colonies in the Tingwall area, where breeding numbers are now falling, failed (Okill 2000b). In Orkney, 48 nests monitored on Egilsay produced only eight chicks (0.17 per nest).

In north-east England, 84 pairs nested on the Farnes. In east England, surveys of islands on the Blackwater Estuary found an estimated 1,200 pairs on Pewet Island (1,500 in 1998) and 309 pairs on Great Cob Island (233 in 1998). At Minsmere, *c.*316 pairs produced between 219 and 238 chicks. At Scolt Head, 1,035 pairs nested, raising a minimum of 1,000 fledglings. In south-east England, numbers at North Solent increased for the second successive year, from 4,977 pairs in 1999 to 6,125 pairs in 2000. Breeding success was again good, with between two and three chicks fledged per pair. On the River Medway, flush counts on Burntwick, Greenborough and Nor Marsh islands found 8,750, 5,000 and 350 individuals respectively, suggesting a substantial increase has occurred here since 1987. Nearby at Elmley RSPB reserve on The Swale, 3,155 apparently incubating adults were counted at Flander's Mare, with a further 350 at Mockett's Saltmarsh. At Rye Harbour, numbers declined from 180 pairs in 1999 to just 33 pairs in 2000. Following complete breeding failure at this site in 1999, between 10-20 chicks fledged in 2000. A similar situation occurred at Dungeness, where productivity from 67 nests was 0.30 young per nest (350 pairs, productivity 0.09 chicks per nest in 1999). In south-west England, 199 breeding pairs on Brownsea Island produced only 10-20 chicks due to predation by common buzzard *Buteo buteo* and great black-backed gull *Larus marinus*.

In Wales, productivity was low at Cemlyn where 150 young fledged from 440 nests (0.34 per nest). In north-east Ireland, numbers were much reduced at Strangford Lough where only 1,706 pairs bred (cf. 3,349 in 1999), well below the 1990-99 mean (5,153, s.d. $\pm$ 1,251). Also in north-east Ireland, 250 pairs nested at Big Copeland, 100 less than in 1999, and 100 pairs bred at Cockle Island.

3.13 Mew gull *Larus canus*

Breeding numbers and breeding success (Table 3.13.1)

In western Scotland, accurate counts have been undertaken annually at 20 breeding sites since 1994 (Table 3.13.1) (Craik 2000). At these sites there was an 8% increase between 1999 and 2000, with numbers the highest recorded since 1995. Mink control efforts were again noticeable in enhancing breeding success. In 2000, at 13 colonies where mink were successfully controlled, 490 chicks fledged from a total of 682 nests (0.72 per pair). This contrasts with 36 colonies (33 with no mink control, three where mink control failed) where a total of 764 pairs fledged 281 chicks (0.37 per pair). Twenty-two of these colonies, holding 265 pairs, failed completely (Craik 2000). Elsewhere in western Scotland, numbers nesting on Handa were similar to 1999, with between 11 and 15 pairs holding territory in 2000. A slight decline was recorded on Sanda, from 44 pairs in 1999, to 38 pairs. On Eigg, 60 pairs held territory and breeding success from a sample of 30 nests was 1.33 chicks per nest.

Table 3.13.1 Numbers of mew gulls in study colonies on the west coast of Scotland 1994-2000. Figures are sums of counts of pairs at 20 colonies in Argyll & Bute and southern Lochaber.

Year	1994	1995	1996	1997	1998	1999	2000	1999-2000 % change
No. of pairs	1,081	1,015	821	805	929	913	986	+8.0

Colonies: Glas Eileanan, Eilean Inshaig, Tucker's Island, Sgeir na Caillich, Eilean an Ruisg, Eilean Mor, Glas Eilean, Kilmaronag, Aird's Point Islet, Bonawe Island, McCormaig Island, Eilean Fada, Ardrishaig, Sanda, Eilean Dubh, Eilean Gainimh, Sgeir Sallachain, Eilean Choinneich, Coruanan, Eilean Nan Gall.

In Shetland, visits to colonies to ring chicks indicated that mew gulls generally had a poor breeding season. The Hildasay colony fledged only ten young and few young fledged at Tingwall, continuing this colony's decline. The colony at Wormadale Hill failed due to feral ferrets eating the chicks, and colonies on Whalsay seemed to do poorly after the June storm (Okill 2000b). On Foula, six pairs were found nesting, identical to the last full count in 1987 (Harvey *et al.* 2000). On Fair Isle, eight pairs fledged an average of 0.75 chicks per pair (Shaw *et al.* 2000). In Orkney, a colony at Kirkbister was very successful, but a colony at Littlequoy had much poorer success than in 1999.

The colony at Nigg in north Scotland continued to increase, to 117 pairs (104 in 1999). Breeding success averaged 1.15 chicks per pair from a sample of 46 monitored nests (1996-99 mean 0.94, s.e. ± 0.12) (Swann 2000b). However, in the same area, the colony at Alness Point decreased to 90 pairs (102 pairs in 1999) with poor productivity averaging only 0.44 chicks per pair (compared to 1.08 in 1999, 1.50 in 1998 and 0.75 in 1997). In north-east Scotland, breeding success in the colony at Bluemill, was considered to be poor, possibly due to cold and dry weather in late June and predation by fox *Vulpes vulpes* and stoat *Mustela erminiea* (I. Francis, pers. comm.).

In north-east Ireland, breeding numbers at Strangford Lough decreased from the high of 138 pairs reached in 1999, to 82 pairs, the lowest figure recorded since 1992 (Andrews *et al.* 2000). At Big Copeland Island, 110 pairs nested, and on Old Lighthouse Island, 14 pairs fledged one chick per pair (N. McKee, pers. comm.). Numbers at these two colonies have remained fairly stable since 1997 and 1994 respectively. In north-west Ireland, 46 pairs nested on Clare Island though disturbance, possibly by sheepdogs, led to 32 nests subsequently suffering predation by great black-backed gulls.

3.14 Lesser black-backed gull *Larus fuscus*

Breeding numbers and breeding success (Table 3.14.1)

In north-west England, the South Walney colony was estimated to hold *c.*18,391 pairs (19,487 in 1999, though census methods differed slightly). For the third successive year, an outbreak of botulism caused substantial adult mortality in late summer (N. Littlewood, pers. comm.). The annual census of the large inland gull colony at Tarnbrook Fell (north-west England) found an estimated total of 18,933 nests with eggs, compared with 17,155 in 1999 and 14,129 in 1998, of which *c.*97-98% were lesser black-backed gulls and the remainder herring gulls (Sowter 2000). However, nests with eggs represented only 56% of the total numbers in sample quadrats and these figures should be treated as minimum population estimates. The estimate of 24,737 pairs cited in the 1999 report (Upton *et al.* 2000) was based on application of a conversion factor as used between 1990 and 1997 to allow for missed and late nests (Coulson, various, in Sowter 2000). Applying the same analysis to the 2000 survey data gives an estimate of 23,818 breeding pairs. Further studies of the relationship between numbers of nests and actual breeding pairs are planned in 2001 (Sowter 2000). Subsequent to the 2000 census, 11,946 birds were culled as part of a long-term water quality management strategy. Breeding success in a small sample plot in 2000 was estimated at 0.89 chicks fledged per nest with eggs (n = 19), somewhat lower than the 1993-96 mean of 1.35, but still sufficient to fuel further growth of the colony despite the cull measures (Sowter 2000). Elsewhere, at Rockcliffe Marsh, the mixed colony of lesser black-backed and herring gulls was estimated to contain 10,320 nesting pairs but fledged under 5,000 chicks. In north-east England, the mixed colony on the Farnes declined by almost 6%, to 1,233 pairs. In east England, breeding numbers at Orford Ness were estimated at 23,000 pairs, an increase of 2.2% on 1999, although 75% of nests failed due to fox predation (D. Cormack, pers. comm.). At Terrington, it was estimated that between 1,378 and 2,096 pairs nested along the outer trial bank. Eggs were pricked at this site for tern conservation purposes.

Table 3.14.1 Population changes at monitored lesser black-backed gull colonies, 1999-2000. Figures are breeding pairs, apparently incubating adults or apparently occupied nests in May-June.

	SW Scotland[a]	SE Scotland[b]	E England[c]	Wales[d]
1998	963 - 1,093	2,193	21,700	16,939
1999	868 – 888	2,118	22,500	16,126
2000	905	1,621	23,000	13,839
1999-2000 % change	+*c.*3%	-23.5	+2.2	-14.2

Colonies: [a] Reisa Mhic Phaidean, Eilean Gamha, Bach Island, Eilean Mor, Eilean Dubh, Eilean na Cille, Eilean Aoghainn, Glas Eilean, Sanda, Lunga; [b] Isle of May, Fidra; [c] Orford Ness; [d] Skomer, Skokholm, Middleholm, Bardsey, Caldey, Elegug Stacks, South Stack.

In Wales, the annual census of breeding numbers on Skomer resulted in an estimated 10,007 pairs, the lowest figure in the period 1986-2000 (Brown & Easton 2000). Breeding success was 0.43 chicks per pair, above the 1989-99 average (0.23, s.e. ± 0.06), but well below the number needed for the population to maintain itself (Perrins 2000). Numbers on adjacent Middleholm increased by 30 pairs from 1999, to 106 pairs. On Skokholm, numbers declined from 1999 by 16.4%, to 2,419 pairs, also the lowest count at this site compared with the previous 14 years. Breeding success was again very poor, at 0.18 chicks fledged per pair. However, further north on Bardsey, numbers increased by 23.4%, to 594 pairs, and breeding success averaged 0.76 chicks fledged per pair, well above the range recorded during 1996-99 (0.26-0.56). An estimated 747 pairs were found nesting on the Skerries, a decline of 36% on the last count of 1,169 pairs in 1993.

In south-west Scotland, *c*.1,153 pairs were found nesting at 22 sites. Of colonies that were counted in 1999 and 2000, numbers were found to have increased by *c*.3% to 905 pairs. The three largest colonies, containing 550 pairs in 1999, accounted for 700 pairs in 2000. At 13 colonies where breeding success was monitored, 926 pairs averaged 0.53 chicks per pair (Craik 2000), very similar to the 1999 figure. In south-east Scotland, the annual census of the gull colony on the Isle of May found an estimated 1,442 nests, a decline of 5.1% on the 1999 figure. Breeding success was 0.98 chicks per pair, well above the 1989-99 average (0.81, s.e. $\pm$ 0.07) (Wilson 2000). On six islands in the Firth of Forth surveyed in both 1999 and 2000, numbers were found to have declined from 1,013 pairs to 502 pairs. In Shetland, no birds were found on territory in the Hildasay colony in early July (Okill 2000b).

In north-east Ireland, a total of 128 pairs nested at Strangford Lough, the lowest count at this site since 1993 (Andrews *et al.* 2000). At Old Lighthouse Island, numbers decreased from 250 pairs in 1999, to 200 pairs, but breeding success was good. Slight increases were noted at Big Copeland Island (310 pairs, cf. 300 in 1998) and Mew Island (50 pairs, cf. 40 in 1999) (N. McKee, pers. comm.).

3.15 Herring gull *Larus argentatus*

Breeding numbers and breeding success (Table 3.15.1)

Few herring gull colonies are counted regularly, but the limited data available suggest that coastal populations were roughly stable or declining between the mid-1980s and mid-1990s, following major declines from the early 1970s to mid-1980s (Walsh & Gordon 1994; Lloyd *et al.* 1991). However, population trends at individual colonies may vary within regions, so that data for small samples of colonies are not necessarily indicative of more widespread changes.

In both north-west and south-west Scotland, overall numbers at regularly monitored colonies increased from 1999 levels. Breeding success across eight colonies at which mink were controlled averaged 1.21 fledglings per pair from *c*.1,637 nests, compared with just 0.79 fledglings per pair for *c*.6,905 nests at 48 colonies of ten or more pairs in which mink were not controlled. At 12 of these latter colonies, where mink were known to be active, only 0.33 chicks fledged per nest from 1,104 pairs and seven colonies completely failed (Craik 2000). On Eigg, numbers increased by 22% to 360 territories from the low number recorded in 1999. On Canna, numbers increased from 1999 levels by 11%, to 1,282 territories, though it was a very poor breeding season with only 0.37 chicks fledged per pair from 176 study nests (Swann 2000a).

In Shetland, the colony on Hildasay failed, possibly due to the June storm. However, colonies at Cunningsburgh and Lerwick both produced good numbers of chicks. At Gulberwick, a number of dead chicks were found and the colony had dwindled to only six pairs by the end of the season (Okill 2000b). Productivity on Noss was also poor due to the June storm, 67 pairs produced only 20 chicks. On Foula, a complete count produced 15 pairs, the same as at the last complete count in 1987. In north Scotland, the colony at Nigg increased from 73 to 208 pairs. Many pairs at this colony now nest on rooftops and it is thought that the 1999 figure underestimated the number of roof nesting pairs. In north-east Scotland, there was some recovery in numbers breeding at Sands of Forvie NNR, to 488 pairs (445 in 1999, 575 in 1998). In south-east Scotland, numbers at St. Abb's Head increased by 21% from 1999, to 307 pairs though this is still low compared to 1978 when 907 pairs nested. The colony on Fidra increased by 23%, from 1,399 pairs in 1999 to 1,716 pairs, but there was little change on the Isle of May, with a decline of 2% to 3,067 nests. Breeding success of 0.64 chicks fledged per pair was near the long-term average.

Table 3.15.1 Population changes at monitored herring gull colonies, 1999-2000 (breeding pairs or apparently occupied nests in May-June). Regional samples < 200 pairs are excluded.

	SW Scotland [a]	NW Scotland [b]	NE Scotland [c]	SE Scotland [d]	E England [e]	Wales [f]	NW England [g]	NE Ireland [h]
1998	2,893	2,995	575	4,458	6,050	3,954	638	575
1999	2,874	2,918	445	4,828	6,250	3,929	602	435
2000	2,917	3,037	488	5,174	6,750	4,644	544	253
1999-2000 % change	+1.5	+4.1	+9.7	+7.2	+8.0	+18.2	-9.6	-41.8

Colonies: [a] Sgeir nan Gobhar, Rubha an Ridrie, Eilean Mor, Eilean Beag, Glas Eilean, Eilean Loch Oscair, Sgeir nan Tom, Eilean Gainimh, Inn Island, Kilmaronag, Abbot's Isle, Eilean nan Caorach and nearby, Ruadh Sgeir, Eiean Eoghainn, Sgat Beag, Sgat Mor, Eilean Buidhe, Sanda, Lunga; [b] Sligneach Mor, An Glas Eilean (Moidart), An Glas Eilean (Arisaig), An Glas Eilean (Loch nan Uamh), Sgeir Glas, Eilean MhicNeill, Sgeir an Eididh, Am Fraoch-eilean, Sgeir an Fheoir, Eilean an Sgurra, Rubha da Chuain, Eilean da Chuain, Eilean Dubh, Eilean Balnagowan, Fort William islets, Canna, Eigg, Handa; [c] Sands of Forvie NNR; [d] Isle of May, Carr Craig, Fidra, Haystack, St. Abb's Head; [e] Orford Ness; [f] Stackpole Head plus Elegug Stacks and nearby, Skomer, Skokholm, Middleholm, St. Margarets, Caldey, Bardsey, South Stack, Yny Gwylan Fawr; [g] St. Bee's Head; [h] Strangford Lough (several colonies).

In east England, the mixed colony at Orford Ness continued its expansion, holding 6,750 breeding pairs of herring gulls, an 8% increase on 1999. However, breeding success was poor with nests suffering 75% fox predation. At Terrington, between 1,004 and 1,544 pairs nested though the eggs were pricked to aid tern conservation. Colonies near Rye Harbour had mixed fortunes: five pairs at the harbour failed though 90 pairs in the village and at North Point had moderate to high breeding success. At Dungeness (south-east England), 102 pairs nested though the majority of these had their eggs destroyed to aid tern conservation. At Burton Bradstock in south-west England, 27 pairs fledged an average of 2.29 chicks per nest, equal to the 1992-98 colony mean.

In Wales, numbers on Skomer declined slightly to 367 pairs (374 pairs in 1999), though on adjacent Middleholm nesting pairs increased to 113 (104 pairs in 1999). Breeding success averaged 0.59 chicks per nest from 37 monitored nests at the former site (Brown & Easton 1999). On Skokholm, 309 pairs nested, the lowest figure at this site since 1991. Breeding success averaged 0.67 chicks per pair from a sample of 124 nests. Since 1999, increases occurred at colonies on South Stack (+122% to 543 pairs), Caldey Island (+30% to 2,134 pairs) and Castlemartin SSSI (+12% to 209 pairs), while the colony on the Skerries was found to have increased by 6% (943 pairs) since the previous count in 1993. Productivity on Bardsey was good, averaging 1.11 chicks per nest from 534 pairs. On nearby Ynysoedd Gwylan, breeding success was also good with 235 pairs producing 0.89 chicks per nest, though 81 large young and 11 adults were found dead, possibly as a result of botulism (Stansfield 2000).

In north-west England, the large mixed colony at South Walney was estimated to hold c.9,600 pairs of herring gulls. A substantial outbreak of botulism in late summer caused significant mortality for the third successive year (N. Littlewood, pers. comm.). The colony at St. Bees Head declined for the second successive year to 544 pairs (cf. 602 pairs in 1999, 638 pairs in 1998). In north-east Ireland, the long-term decline at Strangford Lough continued. Numbers decreased since 1999 by 42% to 253 pairs, the lowest figure recorded in the period 1986-2000 (Andrews et al. 1999). At Old Lighthouse Island, 100 pairs nested but breeding success was poor.

3.16 Great black-backed gull *Larus marinus*

Breeding numbers and breeding success (Table 3.16.1)

A review of the limited available data suggests that coastal populations of great black-backed gulls in the UK generally increased or remained roughly stable between 1986 and 1994 (Walsh & Gordon 1994). However, a survey of the largest British colonies on Hoy (Orkney) in 1996 found that these had declined markedly since 1984 (Furness 1997). Counts on Hoy in 2000 revealed a further reduction of almost 25% since 1996, to 488 pairs.

Table 3.16.1 Population changes at monitored great black-backed gull colonies, 1999-2000 (breeding pairs or apparently occupied nests in May-June). Regional samples of < 50 pairs are excluded.

	SW Scotland[a]	NW Scotland[b]	Shetland[c]	N Scotland[d]	NW England[e]	Wales[f]
1998	294	182	55	104	120	201
1999	315	164	51	134	100	219
2000	371	185	56	139	85	197
1999-2000 % change	+17.8	+12.8	+9.8	+3.7	-15.0	-10.0

Colonies: [a] Sanda, Lunga, Eilean Gainimh, Abbot's Isle, Dubh Sgeir, Ruadh Sgeir, Sgat Mor, Carraig an Daimh, Eilean Buidhe, Eilean na Cille; [b] Eigg, Canna, Sligneach Mor, Handa, Sgeir an Fheoir, An Glas Eilean (Loch nan Uamh), An Glas Eilean (Moidart), Eilean MhicNeill; [c] Noss; [d] Nigg oil terminal; [e] South Walney; [f] Skomer, Skokholm, Middleholm, Stackpole Head plus Elegug Stacks, Caldey, South Stack, Bardsey, Ynys Gwylan.

At monitored colonies in south-west and north-west Scotland, there were increases of 18% and 13% in breeding numbers respectively between 1999 and 2000 (Table 3.16.1). Within Clive Craik's study area, 696 pairs were found at 73 sites, with single pairs at 34 of these. Of those sites where productivity was known, breeding success averaged 1.17 chicks per pair across *c.*677 nests at 63 sites, including single breeding pairs at 27 sites that fledged between 0.93 and 0.96 chicks per pair. There was complete breeding failure at 18 of the monitored sites, with mink probably responsible in ten cases (Craik 2000). On Sanda, numbers declined by 30% from 1999 to 38 pairs, and in late summer many large chicks were found dead, possibly due to a very dry spell of weather (Morton 2000). On Canna, 89 territories were apparently occupied, nine more than in 1999, continuing the long-term increase evident since 1981. Overall productivity from 41 monitored pairs was 1.34 young per pair, close to the 1997 to 2000 average (Swann 2000a). Numbers on Handa (37 territories) and Lunga (67 pairs) remained virtually unchanged from 1999 (cf. 36 territories and 70 pairs respectively).

In Shetland, 56 pairs bred on Noss, fledging 34 chicks (0.61 young per pair) (Upton *et al.* 2000). On Foula, numbers had declined by 36% to 16 pairs since the last full survey in 1987. In Orkney, breeding success at Swona and Mull Head was reported to be back to normal after the very poor year in 1999. In northern Scotland, the colony at Nigg continues to increase and now numbers 149 pairs. An excellent breeding season at this site resulted in 266 chicks fledging from 120 monitored nests, an average of 2.22 young per nest, well above the 1991-99 mean (1.74, s.e. $\pm$ 0.14). Pre-fledging mortality was particularly low with only 16 ringed chicks found dead (Swann 2000b). In south-east Scotland, the population on the Isle of May continued to increase, reaching a new peak of 23 pairs.

In Wales, breeding success improved on 1999 at several sites. On Skomer, productivity from 25 nests was 1.52 young per pair (Brown & Easton 2000). On the Skerries, 14 pairs fledged 17 chicks (1.21 young per pair) and on Skokholm, 53 monitored pairs fledged an average of 1.13 young each. On Ynys Gwylan Fawr, 54 pairs fledged an average of 1.79 chicks per pair and three pairs on

Bardsey fledged 2.33 young per pair (Stansfield 2000). Numbers at the majority of Welsh colonies appeared stable, though at Middleholm, numbers declined from 34 territories in 1999 to 14 territories in 2000.

In north-west England, the colony at South Walney underwent further decline, from 100 pairs in 1999 to 85 pairs. At Rockcliffe Marsh, 39 pairs fledged 0.56 young per pair. Four pairs fledged six young on Brownsea Island (south-west England). In north-east Ireland, numbers declined at Strangford Lough for the second successive year, from 53 to 41 pairs. This is the lowest figure for this site in the period 1986 to 2000 (Andrews *et al.* 2000).

3.17 Black-legged kittiwake *Rissa tridactyla*

Breeding numbers (Table 3.17.1, Figure 3.17.1)

Black-legged kittiwakes may move between colonies and hence, year to year changes in counts of kittiwakes at sample colonies may not always necessarily reflect larger scale regional population changes.

Due to commitments to Seabird 2000, few breeding stations were surveyed in Shetland in both 1999 and 2000. However, data from productivity plots (Table 3.17.1), together with whole colony counts from the three largest stations (Fair Isle, Noss and Foula) suggests that the population is still in decline (Heubeck 2000). A complete count of Fair Isle revealed 8,175 apparently occupied nests (AON), a decrease of 29.8% since the last similar survey in 1997. Numbers declined on Noss by 17.1% to 2,395 AON from 1998. On Foula, a complete census recorded 1,982 nests (including traces), revealing a 10.6% decline since 1999. In Orkney, comparable whole colony counts at Mull Head and Costa Head revealed a 35.1% decrease since 1997, to 1,835 AON, continuing the decline at these colonies over the past decade (Thompson & Walsh, in press). In north-east Scotland, numbers at the Sands of Forvie increased since 1999, by 6% to 601 AON. A complete count of suitable coastline in Moray revealed 488 AON. In south-east Scotland, there was a further recovery in overall numbers following the major decline between 1997 and 1998 (Thompson *et al.* 1999). A total of 11,077 AON were found at St. Abb s Head, compared with 9,576 in 1999 and 8,044 in 1998. This is, however, still some way below the 13,393 AON recorded in 1997. After declines noted in the previous two years, numbers on the Isle of May increased from 1999 by 10.1%, to 4,618 AON. A complete count of islands in the Firth of Forth (Craigleith, The Lamb, Fidra, Inchkeith and Inchcolm) found 1,490 AON, an increase of 13.2% on 1999.

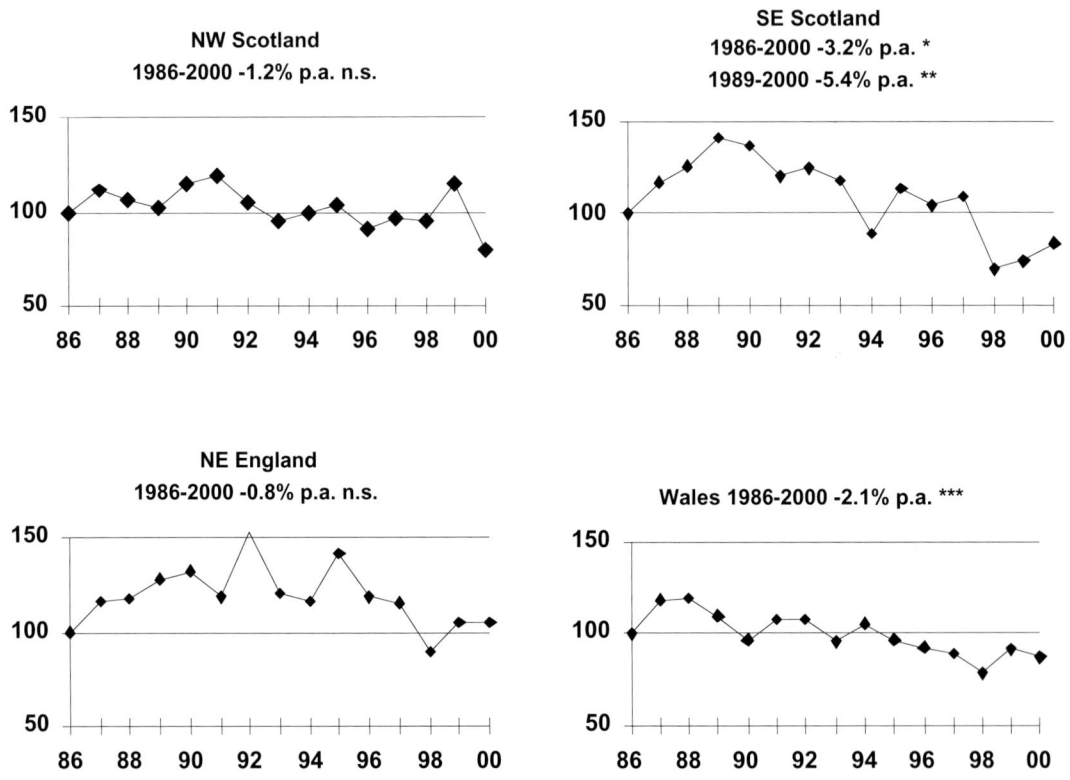

Figure 3.17.1 Sample population indices for breeding black-legged kittiwakes, 1986-2000. Average annual rates of change as shown were calculated by regression of natural log of index against year (see section 1.2.2. for details). Statistical significance of trends (t-test) indicated as: n.s. not significant, * P < 0.05; ** P < 0.01; *** P<0.001.

36

In north-west Scotland, numbers on Canna continue to increase, reaching a new high of 1,274 AON. However, a count of the east coast of neighbouring Rum found just 783 AON, a decrease of 60.3% since 1999.

In north-west England, there was an increase in the population at St. Bees Head for the second successive year, numbers rising by 5.7% to 1,341 AON. On the Farnes (north-east England), the population decreased by 6.7% to 5,125 AON. Elsewhere in this area, numbers increased at Huntcliff by 17% from 1999 to 3,950 AON. In Suffolk, the small colony on the Sizewell rigs, which are fast approaching capacity, was estimated at 180 AON (140 in 1999) (A. Miller pers. comm.). There was again a slight decline at South Foreland (Kent) to 1,676 AON from 1,861 in 1999.

There was a slight increase in numbers on Skomer, from 2,156 AON in 1999 to 2,257. Elsewhere in Wales, the colony at Great and Little Orme increased by 31.7% from 1,313 to 1,729 AON between 1999 and 2000.

Table 3.17.1 Population changes at monitored black-legged kittiwake colonies, 1999-2000 (apparently occupied nests in late May or June) and 1986-99 population trends. Trends for NE Scotland are based on triennial monitoring at Troup\Lion s Head and Bullers of Buchan. Counts with a reported inaccuracy of > 5% and regional samples <500 AON are excluded. Average annual rates of change for 1986-99 were calculated by regression of natural log of index against year (see section 1.2.2. for details). Statistical significance of trends (t-test) indicated as: n.s. not significant, * P<0.05, ** P<0.01, ***P<0.001.

	NW Scotland	Shetland	N Scotland	NE Scotland	SE Scotland
% annual change	1986-99 -0.6 n.s.	1986-99 -9.7**	-	1992-98 -9.4 n.s.	1986-99 -3.2*
1999	1,984	4,134	658	827	14,462
2000	1,974	3,663	447	1,006	16,514
1999-2000 % change	-0.5[a]	-11.4[b]	-32.1[c]	+21.6[d]	+14.2[e]

	NE England	SE England	Wales	NW England	SE Ireland
% annual change	1986-99 -0.7 n.s.	1986-99 -2.2*	1986-99 -2.2*	1986-99 +1.9 n.s.	1986-99 +1.0 n.s.
1999	8,867	1,861	3,251	1,396	907
2000	9,075	1,676	3,272	1,526	835
1999-2000 % change	+2.4[f]	-9.9[g]	+0.6[h]	+9.3[i]	-7.9[j]

Colonies: [a] Canna, Handa (productivity plots); [b] Sumburgh, Noness, Ramna Geo, Westerwick, Noss, Hermaness, Fair Isle (all productivity plots), Foula; [c] North Sutor; [d] Fowlsheugh (plots), Sands of Forvie NNR; [e] Isle of May, Inchkeith, Fidra, Inchcolm, St. Abb's Head; [f] Farne Islands, Saltburn; [g] Fan Bay-West Langdon Cliffs; [h] Elegug Stacks, Skomer, St. Margaret's, Bardsey, South Stack, Little Orme; [i] St. Bee's Head, Peel Hill, Contrary Head-Traie Cronkan; [j] Dunmore East, Portally.

Breeding success (Table 3.17.2, Figure 3.17.2)

Breeding success in 2000 averaged 0.78 (s.e. $\pm$ 0.05) chicks fledged per breeding pair at 40 colonies, compared with the 1986-99 mean of 0.72 (s.e. $\pm$ 0.03) at 30 to 61 colonies annually, and 0.82 (s.e. $\pm$ 0.06) at 43 colonies monitored in 1999. Across 40 colonies monitored in both 1999 and 2000, there was an overall decline in mean breeding success of 0.03 (s.e. $\pm$ 0.06) chicks fledged per breeding pair. However, these overall figures mask marked regional differences.

Table 3.17.2 Black-legged kittiwake breeding success, 1999-2000: estimated number of chicks fledged per occupied, well-built nest at sample colonies (superscript n = number of colonies). Figures are presented as the mean and standard error of figures for individual colonies. Changes in breeding success are indicated for colonies studied in both years (significant changes, as indicated by t-test: * P<0.05, ** P<0.01, ***P<0.001).

| Region | 1999 chicks fledged/nest | | | | 2000 chicks fledged/nest | | | | 1999-00 change | |
	Nests[n]	Range	Mean	$\pm$s.e.	Nests[n]	Range	Mean	$\pm$s.e.	Mean[n]	$\pm$s.e.
SW Scotland[a]	288[1]	-	1.21	-	183[1]	-	0.82	-	-0.39[1]	-
NW Scotland[b]	1,253[3]	0.22-1.22	0.69	$\pm$0.29	1,176[3]	0.38-1.10	0.66	$\pm$0.22	-0.03[3]	$\pm$0.10
Shetland[c]	2,102[9]	0.18-1.31	0.71	$\pm$0.12	1,876[8]	0.00-1.08	0.48	$\pm$0.12	-0.33[8]	$\pm$0.04***
Orkney[d]	1,235[7]	0.75-1.18	1.04	$\pm$0.06	1,250[7]	0.59-1.32	0.89	$\pm$0.10	-0.15[7]	$\pm$0.07
N Scotland[e]	155[1]	-	0.52	-	139[1]	-	0.53	-	+0.01[1]	-
NE Scotland[f]	692[3]	0.11-0.45	0.23	$\pm$0.11	660[3]	0.77-0.98	0.86	$\pm$0.06	+0.63[3]	$\pm$0.05**
SE Scotland[g]	1,457[3]	0.20-0.75	0.52	$\pm$0.16	1,481[3]	0.80-1.14	0.97	$\pm$0.10	+0.45[3]	$\pm$0.17
NE England[h]	1,503[5]	0.76-1.34	0.97	$\pm$0.11	1,025[3]	0.75-1.31	1.04	$\pm$0.16	+0.07[3]	$\pm$0.07
E England[i]	138[1]	-	0.80	-	150[1]	-	0.98	-	+0.18[1]	-
SW England[j]	46[1]	-	0.67	-	49[1]	-	0.99	-	+0.32[1]	-
I. of Man[k]	55[1]	-	0.55	-	78[1]	-	0.75	-	+0.20[1]	-
Wales[l]	1,522[4]	0.69-1.25	0.93	$\pm$0.12	1,634[4]	0.74-1.12	0.86	$\pm$0.09	-0.07[4]	$\pm$0.09
SE Ireland[m]	1,441[4]	0.93-1.55	1.21	$\pm$0.13	1,281[3]	0.16-1.15	0.71	$\pm$0.29	-0.49[4]	$\pm$0.14*
Total	11,887[43]	0.11-1.55	0.82	$\pm$0.06	10,982[39]	0.00-1.32	0.78	$\pm$0.05	-0.03[39]	$\pm$0.06

Colonies: [a] Ailsa Craig; [b] Canna, Handa, St. Kilda; [c] Noness, Hermaness, Eshaness (1999 only), Westerwick, Foula, Noss, Ramna Geo, Sumburgh Head, Fair Isle; [d] Papa Westray, Rousay, Marwick Head, Row Head, Mull Head, Gultak, Costa Head; [e] North Sutor; [f] Bullers of Buchan, Sands of Forvie, Fowlsheugh; [g] Isle of May, Dunbar, St. Abb's Head; [h] Farne Islands, Coquet Island (1999 only), Gateshead-Newcastle, Saltburn, Bempton (1999 only); [i] Lowestoft; [j] Durlston Head-St. Albans Head; [k] Contrary Head-Traie Cronkan; [l] Bardsey, Elegug Stacks, Skomer, Great Orme; [m] Dunmore, Portally (1999 only), Ram Head, Rockabill.

In Shetland, fledging success from eight monitored colonies averaged 0.48 (s.e. $\pm$ 0.12) chicks per AON, far lower than in 1999 (0.74) and below the 1991-99 mean of 0.57 (s.e. $\pm$ 0.09). The lower productivity was apparently due to various factors including the June storm, which occurred too late to allow pairs to relay, predation and lower food availability than in 1999 (Heubeck 2000). At Foula, colonies sheltered by overhangs and located within sea caves were notably more successful as they were afforded some protection from predators and inclement weather (Furness 2000, S. Gear pers. comm.). Productivity on Fair Isle was 1.15 chicks fledged per AON, significantly above the 1986-99 average (0.80, s.e. $\pm$ 0.13). In Orkney, fortunes were mixed at five Mainland colonies. At Mull Head, productivity of 1.35 chicks per AON was the highest on record and at Costa Head productivity of 1.05 chicks per AON was only slightly below that recorded in 1998 and 1999. At Gultak, a productivity of 0.83 chicks per AON was only slightly below average for this site (1989-99 mean =0.88, s.e. $\pm$ 0.08). However, at Marwick Head, only 0.87 chicks were fledged per AON, well below the 1986-99 mean (1.14, s.e. $\pm$ 0.04), and breeding success at Row Head was the poorest on record, with 0.45 chicks fledged per AON. The colony on Rousay fledged 0.55 chicks per AON, the second lowest value recorded here after the complete failure in 1998. On Papa Westray, the Fowlcraig colony produced 1.03 chicks per AON, well above the 1989-99 mean (0.89, s.e. $\pm$ 0.09).

Breeding success along the east coast of Britain was generally good, with the exception of a few sites such as North Sutor (Easter Ross), where breeding success was equal to 1999 at 0.52 chicks per AON (1990-99 mean =0.76, s.e. ± 0.09). Breeding success was good in north-east Scotland where productivity at the Sands of Forvie (0.77 chicks fledged per AON, highest since 1992), Bullers of Buchan (0.82, highest since 1995) and Fowlsheugh (0.98, highest since 1989) was significantly higher than the respective colony averages. In south-east Scotland, conditions for kittiwake breeding on the Isle of May appeared favourable throughout the season. Breeding started earlier than in recent years, with only 8% of pairs initiating nest building not completing nests, and brood neglect was at its lowest level since 1986. Productivity was 0.97 chicks per AON, the highest since 1989 (1986-99 mean =0.52, s.e. ± 0.11) (Bull *et al*. 2000). At St. Abb s Head, 0.80 chicks were produced per AON, slightly above the 1987-99 average (0.73, s.e. ± 0.09) (Rideout & Hall 2000). The colony at Dunbar fledged 1.14 chicks per AON, the highest value recorded since 1992 and well above the 1987-99 average of 0.94 (s.e. ± 0.10).

In north-east England, breeding success was above average on the Farnes (1.05 chicks fledged per AON) and at Gateshead (1.31). At the latter site, the artificial tower next to the Old Baltic Flour Mill again proved successful, with 107 pairs fledging an average of 1.12 chicks per AON. This tower has now been dismantled and is to be re-sited a half mile further downstream before the start of the 2001 breeding season (B. Little, pers. comm.). At Saltburn, productivity of 0.75 chicks per AON was similar to 1999 (0.76), but remained below the long-term average. Further south at Lowestoft (east England), 0.98 chicks fledged per AON, well below the very high 1986-99 mean (1.09, s.e. ± 0.08). In south-west England, the colony at Durlston Head - St. Albans Head, produced 0.99 chicks per AON, an improvement on 1999, but low compared with 1.22 in 1998 and 1.29 in 1997. There was no successful breeding at Berry Head.

In western Scotland, breeding success remained low at all colonies. At St. Kilda, 0.38 chicks fledged per pair, though this was higher than the value recorded in 1999 (0.22). Breeding success was lower than in 1999 on Canna (0.51), Handa (1.10) and Ailsa Craig (0.82). At Canna and Handa, it was the poorest season since 1993 and 1988 respectively (Swann 2000a; Stoneman 2000). Productivity was again exceptionally high at a small sample plot on Colonsay where 1.79 chicks fledged per AON (1.93 in 1999). In Wales, success on Skomer was 0.78, slightly above the long-term average (1986-99 mean 0.72, s.e. ± 0.05). At Elegug Stacks and Bardsey, breeding success of 0.74 and 1.12 chicks per AON respectively represented declines on 1999 figures, though it was still one of the better seasons on record at each site. Success at Great Ormes Head of 0.80 chicks fledged per AON was well above the 1989-99 average of 0.55 (± 0.07). On the Isle of Man, the Peel Hill colony fledged 0.75 chicks per AON, the best year for this site since monitoring started in1997 (A. Moore, pers. comm.).

In south-east Ireland, productivity at Ram Head was the lowest recorded since 1989 at 0.16 chicks per AON. However, the Dunmore colony fledged an average of 0.93 chicks per AON, the second highest figure in the period since 1986. The Rockabill colony was less successful than in 1999, though productivity was still good at 1.15 chicks fledging per AON.

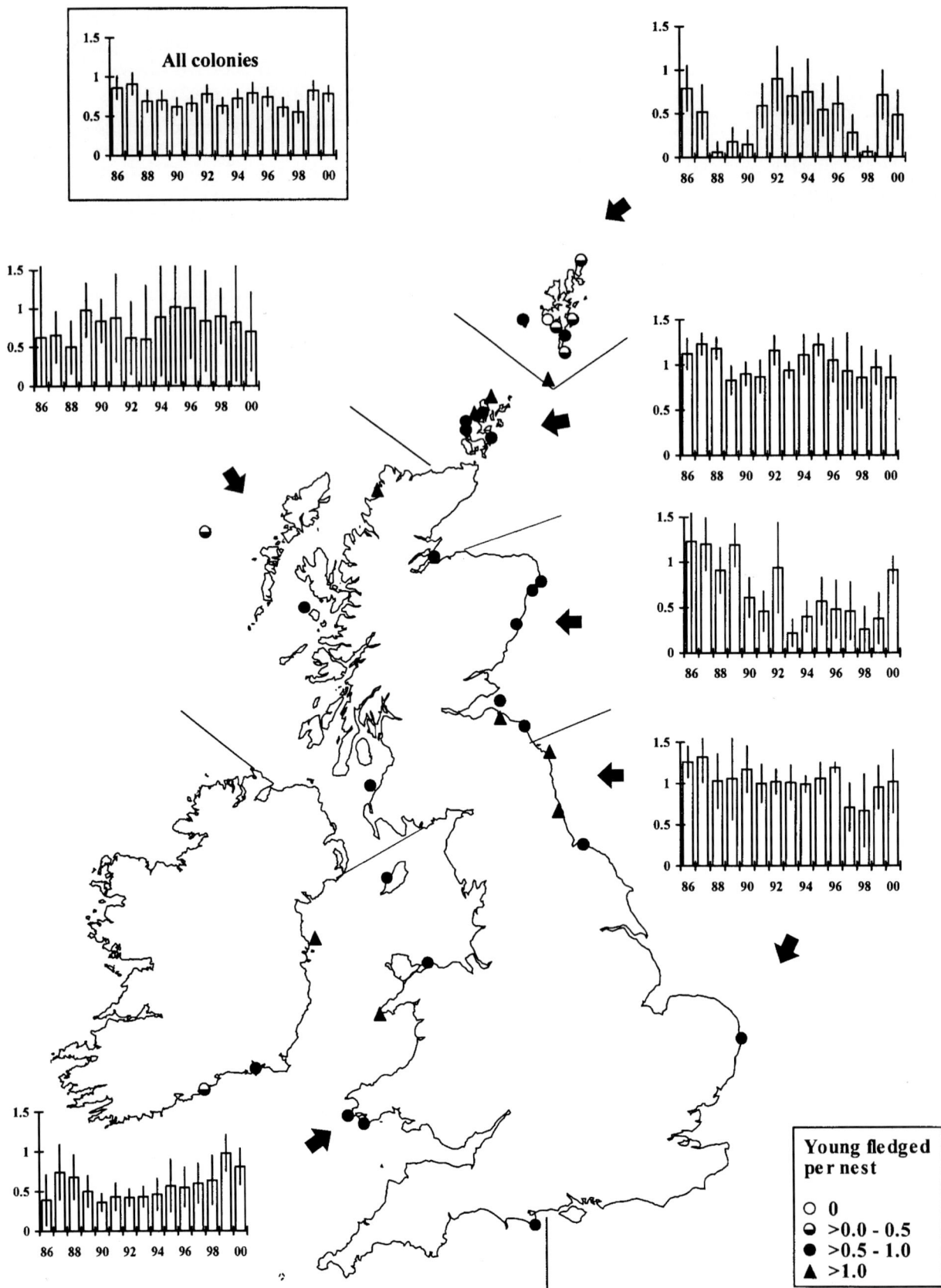

Figure 3.17.2 Breeding productivity (chicks fledged per well-built nest) at black-legged kittiwake colonies during 1986-2000, showing regional and annual variation. Symbols on map represent 2000 figures for individual colonies; histograms show annual averages (with 95% confidence limits) for the regions indicated.

3.18 Sandwich tern *Sterna sandvicensis*

Breeding numbers (Tables 3.18.1 & 3.18.2)

Overall numbers in Britain and Ireland changed little in 2000. Around 70 pairs returned to breed at Loch Ryan, south-west Scotland. In north-east Scotland, there were no breeding pairs at the Loch of Strathbeg, as the breeding island was flooded. Some birds instead moved to the Sands of Forvie, where numbers more than doubled, from 247 to 524 pairs. Increased numbers were also reported from the Isle of May in south-east Scotland, where up to 300 pairs were estimated to have bred (Wilson 2000).

Total numbers on Coquet and the Farnes, north-east England, were little changed in 2000, at 3,676 pairs. In East Anglia, 4,200 pairs bred at Scolt Head (the highest for nearly 30 years) whereas at nearby Blakeney Point numbers fell to *c*.100 pairs, the lowest since 1976. A few pairs also returned to breed at Havergate after a three-year absence. Much of the growth seen in south-east England was due to increased numbers at Burntwick Island (from 155 to 333 pairs), but no birds bred at Rye Harbour in 2000. Although birds returned to Brownsea, south-west England, they did not remain to breed. Some were believed to have bred further along the coast, but exactly where was unknown (C. Williams pers. comm.). The 340 pairs at Hodbarrow, north-west England, were slightly below 1999 levels, but above the ten year mean for the site of 245 pairs (s.d. – 169).

In Wales, there was a 25% decline in the number of breeding birds at Cemlyn, Anglesey to the second lowest level in 15 years. In north-east Ireland, numbers fell from their 1999 high at Larne Lough, to 348 pairs, but increased to 893 pairs at Strangford Lough, the highest level there since 1990. Overall numbers also increased in north-west Ireland, with numbers at Lough Swilly reaching the highest ever recorded at the site, 286 pairs. Numbers fell slightly however, at Lady s Island Lake, south-east Ireland, to 1,005 pairs.

Table 3.18.1 Population changes at monitored Sandwich tern colonies, 1999-2000 (breeding pairs). Trends for 1987-99 are average annual rates of change shown by sample populations. Significance of trends indicated as: n.s. not significant, * $P < 0.05$, ** $P < 0.01$, ***$P<0.001$. Further details of calculation of trends are given in section 1.2.2. Superscript = number of colonies counted in both years.

	SW Scotland	NE Scotland	SE Scotland	NE England	E England	SE England	SW England
1986-1999 annual % change	-	-7.6*	-34.5**	-2.8**	+0.2 n.s.	-4.4***	+9.2**
1999	70	720	116	3,622	4,200	515	174
2000	70	524	c.300	3,676	4,306	689	0
1999-2000 % change	0.0^1	-27.2^2	$+158.6^2$	$+1.5^2$	$+2.5^3$	$+33.8^4$	-100.0^1

	NW England	Wales	NE Ireland	NW Ireland	SE Ireland	Britain & Ireland
1986-1999 annual % change	-7.1**	-2.3 n.s.	-1.0 n.s.	-1.1 n.s.	+4.6 n.s.	-1.7**
1999	380	604	1,814	280	1,048	13,543
2000	340	450	1,902	337	1,005	13,599
1999-2000 % change	-10.5^1	-25.5^1	$+4.9^4$	$+20.4^2$	-4.1^1	$+0.4^{24}$

Table 3.18.2 Numbers of Sandwich tern breeding pairs at regularly counted colonies in Britain and Ireland, 1990-2000 (- indicates that no data were available).

Colony	1990	1991	1992	1993	1994	1995	1996	1997	1998	1999	2000
Loch Ryan	0	14	13	35	60	80	19	0	120	70	70
Loch of Strathbeg	121	283	304	515	923	481	375	355	523	473	0
Sands of Forvie	1126	1115	29	0	0	20	0	4	22	247	524
Isle of May	-	-	0	0	0	0	0	0	2	110	c.300
Long Craig	0	1	40	200	31	4	2	0	0	16	0
Inchmickery	418	473	112	9	98	1	0	0	0	0	0
Coquet Island	1203	1736	2131	1469	1611	1543	1511	1659	1897	1676	1726
Farne Islands	2846	2126	2730	2349	c1750	1837	2179	2484	1785	1946	1950
Scolt Head	0	320	280	853	2406	1588	450	220	650	1000	4200
Blakeney Point	3000	3000	4000	3000	1000	1450	3500	3000	3000	3200	c.100
Minsmere	5	20	0	0	0	23	0	0	0	0	0
Havergate	60	84	70	125	300	250	104	0	0	0	6
Foulness/Maplin	280	280	548	275	405	330	53	36	0	0	0
Dungeness	240	250	250	40	0	0	120	110	0	0	0
Rye Harbour	25	2	0	90	c125	c100	12	c30	13	26	0
Pagham Harbour	26	2	0	0	0	0	0	0	0	0	0
Chichester Harbour	22	5	27	45	9	0	0	0	0	0	0
Langstone Harbour	0	0	0	0	0	0	12	91	158	59	88
North West Solent	150	151	150	85	148	233	173	155	92	275	268
Pitts Deep – Hurst	25	0	90	103	150	2	25	0	-	-	-
Brownsea Island	64	75	82	120	70	107	140	165	c155	174	0
Anglesey	517	601	500	564	400	650	650	450	460	604	450
South Walney	0	0	450	0	0	0	0	0	0	0	0
Foulney	720	332	0	253	380	343	0	0	0	0	0
Hodbarrow	120	520	360	100	0	59	360	230	320	380	340
Larne Lough	130	135	132	c64	152	234	255	253	178	450	348
Green Is., Carlingford	59	172	108	c721	449	270	502	935	c1200	582	650
Strangford Lough	1482	879	657	587	346	532	711	789	389	782	893
Lady's Island Lake	1395	1469	1129	1254	1447	1130	1358	1050	1015	1048	1005
Lough Swilly	109	99	116	119	220	222	240	149	176	259	286
Mulroy Bay	79	76	107	117	23	0	0	0	0	0	0
Lower Lough Erne	45	42	42	51	40	61	56	39	16	21	51
Total	14267	14262	14457	13143	12543	11550	12807	12203	12171	13398	13255

Breeding success (Table 3.18.3)

Productivity was generally good in Britain and Ireland in 2000, with one chick fledged per pair overall. At three colonies in Scotland, overall productivity reached 1.11 chicks per pair. At least 62 chicks were thought to have fledged from 70 pairs at Loch Ryan despite some losses to flooding. At the Sands of Forvie, birds had an excellent season with 1.29 chicks fledged per pair, the highest productivity ever recorded at the site. In south-east Scotland, at least 255 chicks were known to have fledged from up to 300 pairs on the Isle of May.

An estimated 1,100 chicks fledged from 1,950 pairs on the Farnes, north-east England, with no signs of the food shortages of 1999 (Upton *et al.* 2000). In addition, an approximate productivity estimate on Coquet was put at 0.6 fledged per pair. In East Anglia, breeding success at Scolt Head was the highest on record, with about 5,000 fledged from 4,200 pairs. However, herring gull predation at Blakeney resulted in total failure for the 100 pairs there. At North Solent NNR, south-east England, birds had another good year, with an estimated 2.00 chicks fledged per pair from 268 pairs. In addition to the data in Table 3.17.3, at least 23 chicks were known to have fledged from 333 pairs at Burntwick Island, but poor weather delayed the count until late in the season, by which time it was assumed most of the fledged birds had left. At Hodbarrow, north-west England, productivity was 1.18 chicks fledged per pair, well above the ten year mean for the site of 0.40 (s.e. ± 0.17).

On Anglesey, 283 chicks fledged from 450 pairs, the lowest productivity here for at least five years. At Lower Lough Erne, north-west Ireland, a minimum of 35 chicks fledged from 51 pairs. Also in north-west Ireland, 365 large healthy chicks were ringed at Lough Swilly (K. Perry pers. comm.).

Table 3.18.3 Sandwich tern breeding success, 1999-2000: estimated number of chicks fledged per breeding pair at sample colonies (superscript n = number of colonies). When more than one colony was sampled in a given region, the overall figure given is the total number of fledglings divided by the total number of breeding pairs across all colonies. Note that the same colonies have not necessarily been monitored in each region each year and that the numbers of pairs given here are sample sizes (and do not necessarily indicate population changes between years) (- indicates that no data were available).

Region	1999 fledged/pair			2000 fledged/pair		
	pairs^n	Range	overall	pairs^n	range	overall
SW Scotland	-		-	70^1		0.89
NE Scotland	720^2	0.36-0.49	0.40	524^1		1.29
SE Scotland	126^2	0.00-0.50	0.06	$c.300^1$		0.85
NE England	$1,946^1$		0.15	$1,950^1$		$c.0.56$
E England	$4,204^3$	0.00-0.65	0.63	$4,306^3$	0.00-1.19	1.16
SE England	515^4	0.00-1.07	0.65	356^2	0.77-2.00	1.70
SW England	174^1		0.01	-		-
Wales	604^1		0.91	450^1		0.63
NW England	380^1		$c.1.32$	340^1		1.18
NW Ireland	-		-	51^1		>0.69
Total	$8,669^{15}$	0.00-1.32	0.53	$8,347^{12}$	0.00-2.00	1.01

3.19 Roseate tern *Sterna dougallii*

Breeding numbers (Table 3.19.1)

At least 750 pairs bred in the UK and Ireland in 2000. This represents a maximum decline of nearly 5% compared with the 1999 figure of 788 pairs. However, numbers recorded at Lady's Island Lake, south-east Ireland, in 2000 should be considered a minimum figure.

In the UK, numbers fell to 54-55 breeding pairs at eight colonies, from 61 pairs at six colonies in 1999. A further three pairs were seen prospecting around the country. The largest percentage decline occurred in north-east Ireland, where numbers fell to four pairs at Larne Lough after a good year in 1999 when ten pairs nested. In east Scotland, however, the situation looked more promising with the highest number of breeding pairs since 1993, and the number of colonies increasing from one to three. In north-east England, numbers remained stable on Coquet, but declined to just a single pair on the Farnes, the lowest there since monitoring began in 1986. Numbers also remained very low in Wales. The first year of a project to encourage roseate terns to return to breed on the Isles of Scilly, using tape lures and decoys, was not successful in attracting roseates to the site (Robinson & Colombé 2000).

In south-east Ireland, numbers continued to increase at Rockabill, albeit only slightly, from 611 to 618 pairs, with an early season reported. Of those birds whose origins were identified, 89% were recruited from Rockabill, and the largest cohort (19%) were ringed as chicks in 1992 (Crowe *et al.* 2000). At least 78 nests were present at Lady's Island Lake on 15 June.

Table 3.19.1 Roseate tern numbers (breeding pairs) at most colonies during 1989-2000, and breeding success (chicks fledged per pair) in 2000. (- indicates that no data were available)

Region: Colony	1989	1990	1991	1992	1993	1994	1995	1996	1997	1998	1999	2000	Chicks per pair 2000
E Scotland:													
Inchmickery	5	0	0	0	0	2	0	0	0	0	0	0	
Forth B	-	15	23	17	17	7	11	7	8	8	9	10-11	c.0.38
Forth C	-	-	-	-	-	-	1	1	0	0	0	1	0.00
New colony	0	0	0	0	0	0	0	0	0	0	0	1	-
NE England:													
Farne Islands	12	4	3	4	3	2-3	2	2	3	3	4	1	1.00
Coquet Island	25	23	20	29	c30	c38	38	24	25	29	34	34	0.97
New colony	0	0	0	0	0	0	1	14	2	3	0	0	
Wales													
Anglesey A	70	35	1	0	16	18	10	1	2	3	3	2	0.00
Anglesey B	19	7	0	0	0	0	0	0	1	0	0	0	
Anglesey C	9	3	4	7	5	2	0	0	0	2-3	0	0	
NE Ireland:													
Larne Lough	37	19	4	3	0	4	7	13	7	3	10	4	0.00
Carlingford L.	25	3	0	0	0	0	0	0	2	0	0	0	
SE Ireland													
Rockabill	194	321	366	378	427	394	554	557	602	578	611	618	1.52
Lady's Island	76	60	56	76	76	140	60	120	48	80	116	>78	-
TOTAL*	470	490	450	520	578	614	686	744	703	712	788	>750	1.45

* includes pairs noted at other sites in the UK and Republic of Ireland.

Breeding success (Table 3.19.1)

Overall breeding success in Britain and Ireland was again good, with 1.45 young fledged per pair, the highest productivity since 1993. At Forth B, east Scotland, significant failures occurred at the laying stage in early June, and only four young fledged (Jones 2000). Birds on Coquet, north-east England, fledged 33 young from 34 pairs for the second year running.

At Rockabill, south-east Ireland, breeding success was estimated as 1.52 chicks per pair (n = 192), continuing the run of high productivity at this site. Sandeels predominated in the diet and all indications were that food availability was good. No productivity data were available for Lady's Island Lake, but 21 fledglings ringed there were later sighted at Rockabill (Crowe *et al.* 2000).

3.20 Common tern *Sterna hirundo*

Breeding Numbers (Table 3.20.1)

Numbers at UK and Ireland colonies monitored in both 1999 and 2000 changed little overall. A total of 1,269 pairs at 19 colonies were recorded in the study area covered by the mink-seabird project in west Scotland (1,198 pairs at 14 colonies in 1999), including 768 pairs at the largest colony near Mull (Craik 2000). Numbers on the Treshnish Isles also increased, from two to 63 pairs. Numbers fell in north Scotland, largely because no birds bred at McDermott's. However, 203 pairs bred at Nigg, the highest level for five years. Numbers also fell slightly in north-east Scotland, with the main decline occurring at the Loch of Strathbeg, down from 146 to 84 pairs. In south-east Scotland, numbers remained stable overall. On the Isle of May, numbers were the third highest on record, despite a decline of c.25% to 303 pairs (Wilson 2000), while at nearby Leith Docks, the colony increased to its second highest ever level, up from 518 to 690 pairs.

The decline seen in north-east England was entirely attributable to numbers falling at the ICI site at Teesmouth, from 310 to 200-250 pairs (R.Ward, pers. comm.). In East Anglia, only c.50 pairs bred at

Blakeney, but 300 pairs were recorded at Scolt Head, the highest for over 20 years. Sites at Blackwater, Essex, also showed an increase in numbers, from 25 to 72+ pairs. Unfortunately, data were only available for a few central England colonies, and so are unlikely to provide a reliable regional picture. The decrease seen in south-east England was mainly attributable to a decline of over 60% at Dungeness, to 60 pairs, the second lowest on record. On the Isles of Scilly, south-west England, numbers were believed to have been low (Robinson & Colombé 2000), but they remained stable in the region as a whole.

In Wales, numbers at Shotton and the Skerries continued to increase, the Shotton colony having undergone an almost three-fold increase in size since 1975, to 489 pairs. In addition, 13-14 'commics' were reported at Inland Sea. In north-east Ireland, numbers also reached record levels at Green Island, Carlingford, with 509 breeding pairs. Elsewhere in the region, levels remained high at Larne Lough, 521 pairs, and about average at Strangford, 554 pairs. In south-east Ireland, numbers on Rockabill were similar to those in 1999, with 605 pairs (Crowe *et al.* 2000). No data were available for Lady's Island Lake or Dublin Port.

Table 3.20.1 Population changes at monitored common tern colonies, 1999-2000 (breeding pairs). Superscript = number of colonies counted in both years.

	NW & SW Scotland	N Scotland	NE Scotland	SE Scotland	NE England	E England	Central England
1999	1,233	504	386	<1,200	1,863	648	128
2000	1,344	448	355	1,242	1,791	703	181
1999-2000 % change	$+9.0^{28}$	-11.1^{3}	-8.0^{8}	$+3.5^{6}$	-3.9^{11}	$+8.5^{16}$	$+41.4^{7}$

	SE England	SW England	NW England	Wales	Great Britain	NE Ireland	SE Ireland
1999	628	210	60	638	7,498	1,569	610
2000	492	c.210	70	669	7,512	1,601	605
1999-2000 % change	-21.7^{7}	0.0^{2}	$+16.7^{2}$	$+4.9^{4}$	$+0.2^{91}$	$+2.1^{6}$	-0.8^{1}

Breeding success (Table 3.20.2)

Breeding success was generally good in 2000, with productivity above that needed to maintain the population in the majority of regions. In Britain as a whole, productivity reached 1.09 chicks per pair, 65% higher than the 1990-99 mean (0.66, s.e. ± 0.05). Colonies in north-west Scotland, north-east England and Wales had an exceptionally good year, with over one chick fledged per pair, while in south-east Ireland breeding success was also very good at Rockabill.

Overall productivity was moderate at sites in the seabird-mink project study area in western Scotland (*c.*0.71 chicks per pair), but the apparent effectiveness of mink control was not as clear-cut as in previous years due to severe otter predation at two sites where mink had been controlled (Glas Eileanan, Sound of Mull: 768 pairs fledged 100-150, Torinturk: 75 pairs fledged *c.*12). Three colonies were naturally free of mink and birds there were very successful: 45 pairs fledged 84 young (Craik 2000). Flooding caused heavy losses at two other sites in south-west Scotland. In north Scotland, breeding success at Nigg was high for a third successive year, with 267 young fledged from 203 pairs (Swann 2000b). However, at Alness Point, disturbance led to 245 pairs fledging only 45 chicks. Birds in north-east Scotland had another poor year. Heavy predation and either bad weather or a lack of available food were cited as the reasons for failure at the largest monitored colony at St. Fergus, where only 17 young fledged from 118 pairs. Nearby, the Loch of Strathbeg did little better, with 84 pairs fledging 17 young. Although some birds experienced failure at the egg stage at Long

Craig, south-east Scotland, productivity still reached about one chick per pair. At the Isle of May, 399 'commics' fledged, a productivity of 0.33 young per 'commic' pair.

Birds on Coquet and the Farnes, north-east England, had a very successful year, with an estimated 2.20 (n = 22) and 1.33 chicks fledged per pair respectively. In east England, overall success was moderate, with productivity levels varying across the region: 128 pairs at Breydon Water fledged 250 young, whereas all 99 pairs at Snettisham failed, for reasons unknown. The situation was similar in south-east England, with up to one chick per pair at North Solent (123 pairs) and 1.33 chicks per pair at Newtown, Isle of Wight, (four pairs), but a total failure for 57 pairs at Rye Harbour. Bad weather delayed fledgling counts at Burntwick and Greenborough Islands, Kent, so accurate productivity assessments were not possible. In south-west England, great black-backed gull predation resulted in a productivity of $c.0.51$ chicks per pair at Brownsea, but 37 pairs at Lodmoor managed to fledge 45 young. Productivity on the Isles of Scilly was thought to have been low.

The Welsh colonies were again very successful; birds at both Ynys Feurig and the Skerries fledged more than two chicks per pair, and 489 pairs at Shotton fledged 1.16 chicks each. Productivity at Rockabill, south-east Ireland was again high, equalling the ten year average for the region (1.54, s.e. ± 0.18).

Table 3.20.2 Common tern breeding success, 1999-2000: estimated number of chicks fledged per breeding pair at sample colonies (superscript n = number of colonies). When more than one colony was sampled in a given region, the overall figure given is the total number of fledglings divided by the total number of breeding pairs across all colonies. Note that the same colonies have not necessarily been monitored in each region in each year. Numbers of pairs given here are sample sizes and are not necessarily indicative of population changes between years (- indicates that no data were available).

Region	1999 fledged per pair			2000 fledged per pair		
	Pairs[11]	range	overall	pairs[11]	range	overall
SW Scotland	1,051[9]	0.00-3.00	0.65	1,186[11]	0.00-2.33	0.64
NW Scotland	154[6]	0.00-2.00	0.22	79[5]	0.00-3.00	1.65
N Scotland	504[3]	0.00-1.36	0.58	448[2]	0.18-1.32	0.70
NE Scotland	357[7]	0.00-1.00	0.27	269[6]	0.14-1.10	0.36
SE Scotland	227[2]	0.41-1.02	>0.73	75[1]		0.99
Total Scotland	2,293[27]	0.00-3.00	0.57	2,057[25]	0.00-3.00	0.67
NE England	1,270[9]	0.07-2.50	1.00	1,263[6]	0.07-2.20	1.99
E England	625[10]	0.00-1.89	1.29	780[7]	0.00-1.50	0.77
C England	257[15]	0.00-2.80	1.05	-		-
SE England	518[5]	0.00-1.17	0.51	369[5]	0.00-1.33	<0.75
SW England	306[3]	0.36-2.28	0.58	c.210[2]	c.0.51-1.22	0.60
NW England	211[2]	0.74-1.25	0.83	70[2]	0.23-0.50	0.39
Total England	3,187[44]	0.00-2.80	0.90	2,692[22]	0.00-2.20	1.32
Wales	638[4]	0.53-1.74	1.34	637[3]	1.16-2.50	1.44
Total Great Britain	6,118[75]	0.00-3.00	0.82	5,386[50]	0.00-3.00	1.09
SE Ireland	799[2]	1.43-1.81	1.72	605[1]		1.53

3.21 Arctic tern *Sterna paradisaea*

Breeding numbers (Table 3.21.1)

With the end of the ten-year project to monitor breeding success in Shetland and Orkney in 1999, many fewer data were available for these island groups in 2000. There was a severe storm on 12/13 June, which may have caused the loss of many nests at exposed sites in Shetland, but this is not thought to have affected the following data. In Shetland, whole island counts were made on Fetlar, 98 pairs, down from 371 pairs in 1999 (Smith & Luxford 2000), Noss, 29 nests (Upton & Maher 2000), Foula, *c.*800 pairs (Furness 2000) and Fair Isle, 1,251 pairs, similar to 1995-98 levels (Shaw *et al.* 2000). In addition, 17 nests were counted at Hermaness, Unst (Rodger 2000) and *c.*65 pairs bred at a site on Bressay (Upton & Maher 2000). The Dalsetter colony, Mainland, continued to increase in size, to up to 4,000 pairs (S. Croft, pers. comm.). In Orkney, just 683 pairs (assuming 1.5 adults per pair, Bullock & Gomersall 1981) were recorded at North Hill, Papa Westray, a third of the usual figure. On the rest of Papa Westray, there were an estimated 281 adults, and a further 415 birds nested on the neighbouring Holm of Papay (Meek 2000). Although "good numbers" returned to Auskerry at the beginning of the season, only 26 individuals remained to breed (C. Booths, pers. comm.), compared to 1,500 in 1999. A whole-island count of North Ronaldsay found a total of 256 adults.

Overall numbers increased in most other regions in 2000. In west Scotland, 361 pairs at 14 colonies were monitored as part of the mink-seabird project (Craik 2000) compared with 175 pairs at 13 colonies in 1999. Numbers at seven other sites in south-west Scotland declined by 7.6% to 524 pairs, with the most notable decline occurring on the Treshnish Isles, down from 153 pairs to two. At three further sites in north-west Scotland, numbers increased by 80%, to 298 pairs, including a record 130 pairs on the Isle of Eigg. In north Scotland, overall numbers recovered somewhat at three sites, but in north-east Scotland they fell slightly. This was mainly due to numbers falling by 43% at St. Fergus, to 184 pairs, well below the ten year average of 363 (s.d. ± 101). Numbers did increase, however, by 50% at Kinloss, to *c.*223 pairs. The increase in breeding numbers seen in south-east Scotland was due to numbers rising by 23% on the Isle of May, to 908 pairs, the highest ever recorded (Wilson 2000).

The overall increase seen in north-east England was largely because numbers at Long Nanny, Northumberland, reached their highest ever level, up 45% to 1,200 pairs, and numbers also recovered slightly on the Farnes, to 1,526 pairs (Walton 2000). A total of ten pairs bred at three sites in East Anglia, and 33 pairs bred on Foulney, Cumbria, continuing the long-term decline at this site. In Wales, numbers continued their upward trend at both Ynys Feurig and the Skerries, to 335 and 1,368 pairs respectively. This follows several highly productive years at both sites. A further 13-14 'commics' were reported from Cemlyn. In north-east Ireland, numbers at Big Copeland remained stable at 650 pairs. Elsewhere in the region, numbers recovered somewhat from the 1999 low at Strangford Lough and Cockle Island, to 54 and 56 pairs respectively (Andrews *et al.* 2000). Numbers remained stable on Rockabill, south-east Ireland, at 88 pairs. No data were available for Lady's Island Lake.

Table 3.21.1 Population changes at monitored Arctic tern colonies, 1999-2000 (breeding pairs). Superscript = number of sites counted in both years. Regional samples <100 pairs not included.

	NW & SW Scotland	N Scotland	NE Scotland	SE Scotland	NE England	Wales	NE Ireland
1999	909	128	658	740	2,883	1,430	686
2000	1,192	159	619	909	3,559	1,705	766
1999-2000 % change	+31.1[29]	+24.2[3]	-5.9[6]	+22.8[2]	+23.4[3]	+19.2[3]	+11.7[4]

Breeding success (Table 3.21.2)

Generally, breeding success increased in many regions in 2000, although productivity still remained below that needed to maintain the population in most areas. In Shetland, the severe storm of 12/13 June would have ended breeding attempts at exposed sites. However, due to the cessation of the ten year monitoring project, productivity was monitored only at a few sites in Shetland and Orkney in 2000 and so information on the effects of this storm is lacking. Overall productivity at seven sites in Shetland reached 0.52 chicks per pair. Productivity on Fair Isle was the highest ever recorded, with 1,251 pairs fledging approximately 1,000 young. In contrast, all 98 pairs on Fetlar failed, continuing the run of poor productivity here. Inclement weather in June was the probable cause, with young appearing to die of starvation in their first week. On Foula, 150 chicks were seen fledged in the first week of July. In Orkney, at least 107 chicks fledged from 683 pairs at the North Hill RSPB reserve. Productivity was only a little higher than this at other sites on Papa Westray and on the Holm of Papay, with 0.27 and 0.29 fledged per pair respectively (Meek 2000).

In the mink-seabird project study area, west Scotland, the overall productivity of 361 pairs reached 0.70 per pair, with most young fledging from two colonies that were naturally free of mink: Ormsa and Fladda. It was therefore difficult to assess the effectiveness of mink control measures at other sites (Craik 2000). Elsewhere in north-west Scotland, severe rat and some buzzard predation on the Isle of Eigg resulted in 130 pairs fledging just 15 young. Although birds at Nigg, north Scotland, had one of their most successful breeding seasons, with 69 pairs fledging 56 chicks, there were complete failures at McDermott's and Alness Point. Productivity remained low in north-east Scotland. On the Isle of May, south-east Scotland, 0.33 'commic' chicks were estimated to have fledged per nest. This was twice the 1999 figure.

Table 3.21.2 Arctic tern breeding success, 1999-2000: estimated number of chicks fledged per breeding pair at sample colonies (superscript n = number of colonies). When more than one colony was sampled in a given region, the overall figure given is the total number of fledglings divided by the total number of breeding pairs across all colonies. Note that the same colonies have not necessarily been monitored in each region each year and that numbers of pairs given here are sample sizes (and do not necessarily indicate population change between years). (- indicates no data were available)

Region	1999 chicks fledged/pair			2000 chicks fledged/pair		
	Pairs^n	range	Overall	pairs^n	range	overall
Shetland	5,229^{36}	0.00-0.95	0.29	2,259^7	0.00-0.80	>0.52
Orkney	4,511^{29}	0.00-1.10	0.10	1,161^4	0.16-0.29	0.21
SW Scotland	241^7	0.00-1.00	0.36	391^{10}	0.03-1.80	0.65
NW Scotland	72^3	0.00-2.00	0.28	131^2	0.12-2.00	0.13
N Scotland	128^3	0.00-0.33	0.20	159^3	0.00-0.81	0.35
NE Scotland	659^7	0.00-0.63	0.22	484^4	0.04-1.00	0.18
SE Scotland	740^2	0.00-0.15	0.15	1^1		0.00
NE England	2,883^3	0.01-0.70	0.30	2,359^2	1.02-1.30	1.12
E England	18^2	0.50-0.63	0.61	1^1		1.00
Wales	1,457^3	0.00-1.40	1.34 max	1,703^2	1.39-1.49	c.1.41
NW England	34^1		0.29	33^1		c.0.58
NE Ireland	650^1		≥1.00	-		-
SE Ireland	93^2	1.04-1.50	c.1.06	88^1		c.1.39
Total	16,715^{100}	0.00-2.00	0.35 max	8,770^{38}	0.00-2.00	0.80

Overall fledging success was the highest ever recorded in north-east England, with 1.02 and 1.30 (n = 29) chicks fledged per pair respectively at the Farnes and Coquet. In addition, 25 pairs of 'commics' on Lindisfarne fledged 11 chicks. Despite fox predation at Foulney, north-west England, 33 pairs fledged 15-23 young. Birds in Wales had their second most successful season since 1990; 1,368 pairs fledged 1,800-2,000 chicks on the Skerries, and 500 chicks were estimated to have fledged from 335 pairs at Ynys Feurig. In south-east Ireland, productivity was estimated as 1.39 chicks per pair at Rockabill.

3.22 Little tern *Sterna albifrons*

Breeding numbers (Table 3.22.1)

The total number of breeding birds at 57 monitored colonies in Great Britain fell by 8%, to 1,483 pairs. This follows on from the 29% increase seen between 1998 and 1999 (Upton *et al.* 2000). Three pairs bred in Orkney, two fewer than in 1999. At 14 colonies in the rest of Scotland, overall numbers declined by 18%, with the largest decreases occurring at the Sands of Forvie in the north-east, and on Gunna, Tiree, in the south-west. However, despite falling 31% to 51 pairs, numbers at Forvie were more than double the 1985-99 average and this remains the largest monitored colony in Scotland. Numbers dwindled further in south-east Scotland, where two pairs were recorded from only one site.

Just one pair bred at Crimden Dene, the largest colony in north-east England in 1999, but they failed early. This site's abandonment in 2000 was possibly a result of 1999's total failure due to egg theft and crow predation. Some Crimden birds were seen breeding at other colonies along the east coast (R. Wilson pers. comm.), but overall numbers in the region decreased by 18%. The largest decline in east England occurred at Orford Ness, down from 109 to 65 pairs. However, this was more than compensated for by increases at Hamford Water and Blackwater. Great Yarmouth remained the largest colony in the UK, with a total of 220 nests. The most notable declines in south-east England occurred at North Solent, from 23 to two pairs, and at Rye Harbour, which was abandoned (24 pairs in 1999), although eight pairs did nest at another site along the coast. Hayling Oysterbeds continued to attract re-lays from nearby Langstone Harbour, and there were a total of 108 pairs at the two sites, compared to 97 pairs in 1999. Numbers remained stable at Chesil, south-west England.

Although numbers declined by 13% at the Welsh colony, to 75 pairs, they remained higher than the 15-year average for the site (57 pairs, s.d. ± 17). Twenty-six pairs nested at Hodbarrow, north-west England, and up to ten pairs, thought to be Hodbarrow re-lays (N.Holton pers. comm.), bred at nearby Haverigg. Numbers remained low at Kilcoole, south-east Ireland, at 20 pairs (Wilson *et al.* 2000).

Table 3.22.1 Population changes at monitored little tern colonies, 1999-2000 (breeding pairs). Regional samples < 40 pairs are excluded. Superscript = number of colonies counted in both years (including known colonies not occupied in 1999-2000).

	Scotland	NE England	E England	SE England	SW England	Wales	NW England	Great Britain
1999	175	201	820	190	85	86	56*	1,613
2000	144	164	c.807	161	81	75	51	1,483
1999-2000 % change	-17.7[14]	-18.4[10]	-1.6[16]	-15.3[11]	-4.7[1]	-12.8[1]	-8.9[4]	-8.1[57]

* 1998 & 1999 figures inaccurately reported in *Upton et al.* 2000: 1998 total should have stated 30 pairs and the 1999 total 40 pairs, at 3 colonies

Breeding success (Table 3.22.2*)*

Productivity was below 1999 levels in all regions in 2000. Reasons given for failure were inclement weather, flooding, predation and localised food shortages. Only in Wales and south-east Ireland did overall productivity reach levels required to maintain the breeding population.

Overall breeding success in Scotland equalled the 1986-99 average (0.39, s.e. ± 0.06). Although breeding success at Forvie (0.37 fledged per pair) was well below 1998 and 1999 levels, it was still just above the 1987-99 average for the site. Once again, birds in south-east Scotland experienced total failure. Elsewhere in Scotland, at least ten chicks fledged from 33 pairs on Tiree, south-west Scotland, and eight pairs at two sites in the north fledged five. In Orkney, one chick fledged from three pairs.

Table 3.22.2 Little tern breeding success, 1999-2000: estimated number of chicks fledged per breeding pair at sample colonies (superscript n = number of colonies). When more than one colony was sampled in a given region, the overall figure given is the total number of fledglings divided by the total number of breeding pairs across all colonies. Note that the same colonies may not necessarily have been counted in each region each year and that numbers of pairs given here are sample sizes (and do not necessarily indicate population changes between years).

Region	1999 chicks fledged/pair			2000 chicks fledged/pair		
	Pairs[n]	Range	overall	pairs[n]	range	overall
SW Scotland	36[1]		0.58	33[1]		>0.30
N Scotland	-		-	8[2]	0.60-0.67	0.62
NE Scotland	69[2]	0.97-1.00	0.97	53[2]	0.37-2.00	0.43
SE Scotland	5[2]		0.00	2[1]		0.00
Scotland	110[5]	0.00-1.00	0.81	96[6]	0.00-2.00	>0.40
NE England	198[8]	0.00-0.92	0.57	164[10]	0.00-0.44	0.24
E England	650[12]	0.00-2.04	0.79	c.748[19]	0.00-1.67	0.29
SE England	190[8]	0.00-2.17	0.43	142[7]	0.00-0.80	0.25
SW England	85[1]		0.47	81[1]		c.0.27
Wales	86[1]		1.28	75[1]		0.76
NW England	40[2]	0.00-0.46	≥0.15	36[2]	0.00-0.08	0.06
England & Wales	1,249[32]	0.00-2.17	0.69	1,246[40]	0.00-1.67	0.30
Total (GB)	1,359[37]	0.00-2.17	0.70	1,342[46]	0.00-2.00	0.31
SE Ireland	19[1]		2.32	20[1]		1.90

Overall productivity in north-east England was the third lowest recorded since 1986 (1986-99 mean = 0.50, s.e. ± 0.06), with poor weather cited as the main cause of failure. In east England, severe kestrel *Falco tinnunculus* predation was responsible for just 36 young fledging from 220 pairs at Great Yarmouth. A short research project investigating the effectiveness of supplementary feeding in reducing predation rates did not reach an unequivocal conclusion (Smart & Ratcliffe 2000). Very localised food shortages at two sites on the north Norfolk coast resulted in just 30 chicks fledged from 173 pairs. The only sites reporting good productivity in the region were Hamford Water (c.1.00 fledged per pair from 113 pairs) and Havergate (1.67 per pair from three pairs). The largest colony in south-east England, Langstone Harbour, experienced the lowest breeding success since 1993, with just seven young fledging from 97 pairs. Once again, gulls and larger tern species forced birds to nest on shingle areas much more prone to tidal and storm flooding. In addition, there were long periods of continuous rainfall (C.Cockburn pers.comm.). However, 24 pairs re-laid at nearby Hayling Oysterbeds and a total of 35 pairs at this site fledged 27-29 young. Birds at Swale NNR were also reported as fledging good numbers (R.Smith pers. comm.), but there was a total breeding failure at five further sites.

Breeding success at Chesil Bank, south-west England, was about 0.27 chicks per pair, continuing the run of low productivity at this site. Birds in north-west England also had an exceptionally bad year, with just two chicks known fledged from *c.*36 pairs. However, productivity of re-lays at Haverigg was unknown. In Wales, despite periods of bad weather and a high level of egg predation by foxes, 75 pairs fledged 57 young (Jones *et al.* 2000). Productivity at Kilcoole, south-east Ireland, was again very high, with 20 pairs fledging 38 chicks (Wilson *et al.* 2000).

3.23 Common guillemot *Uria aalge*

Breeding numbers (Table 3.23.1, Figure 3.23.1)

For most regions, numbers of adult common guillemots attending breeding ledges at monitored colonies increased from 1999 to 2000. However, it is possible that the large number of common guillemots killed in the oil-spill resulting from the *Erika* in December 1999 may have an affect on future population levels. Over 31,000 dead common guillemots were collected, though the true number killed may be as high as 51,000. Of those collected, rings were recovered from 60, 90% of which were found to have come from colonies around the Irish Sea and west Scotland. Furthermore, 72% of ringed birds were immatures and juveniles, so the full extent of any impacts at British and Irish colonies may not be evident for some time (Mead & Wernham 2000).

In Wales, overall numbers of birds in sample plots decreased and the increase in whole-colony counts was less than the annual average. For individual colonies, decreases in whole colony counts were recorded at Elegug Stacks (-14.3%) and Stackpole Head (-10.7%), but numbers on Skomer increased by 14.1% to 13,852 (cf.12,135 in 1999), the highest count since monitoring began in 1963. Increases in sample plots on Skomer (+3.7%) and South Stack (+3.0%), and decreases at Elegug Stacks (-5.8%) and Skokholm (-7.0%) were not statistically significant. A significant decrease was recorded at Stackpole Head (-29.0%, t=4.593, d.f. =18, P<0.01) though this is rather a small colony. Numbers again increased at St. Bees Head (north-west England), where the whole-colony count of 7,340 birds was 3.1% up on 1999, the previous highest recorded count in the period since 1986. In south-west England, a whole colony count at Berry Head totalled 1,029 birds.

In south-east Scotland, numbers on the Isle of May increased by 24.7%, to 27,045 individuals, bringing numbers back in line with pre-1999 figures. Poor adult attendance is suspected to have been the cause of the unusually low population figure in 1999 (Hemsley 1999). Sample plot counts also increased significantly on the Isle of May (+33.1%, d.f. =18, P<0.001) and at St. Abb's Head (+38.6%, t=11.005, d.f. =11, P<0.001). Large increases were also recorded on the Bass Rock (+47.4% to 3,570), Craigleith (+68.5% to 2,878) and Fidra (+71.0% to 643) though the population on The Lamb decreased (-32.9% to 2,523). In north-east England, numbers increased on the Farnes by 5.3% to 33,038 birds, after two successive years of decline. In north-east Scotland, sample plot counts increased by 1.2%.

In Shetland, sample plot counts at Sumburgh Head increased significantly for the second successive year (+16.5%, t=3.559, d.f. =8, P<0.01). There were also significant increases in plot counts at Troswick Ness (+14.6%, t=3.369, d.f. =8, P<0.01) and on Fair Isle (+19.1%, t=4.215, d.f. =13, P<0.01). Non-significant increases occurred in plot counts at Eshaness (+8.8%), Noss (+3.7%) and Burravoe (+3.5%). At Hermaness there was a non-significant decrease of -2.7% in plot counts while a whole colony count recorded 10,439 birds, a decline of 22.4% since the last complete count in 1996. This decline is mirrored at the monitoring plots, in which numbers have decreased by 15% over the same period. A whole colony count of Foula recorded 41,435 birds, which represents an increase of 10.6% since the last complete survey in 1987.

Table 3.23.1 Population changes at monitored common guillemot colonies, 1999-2000 (adults attending colony in first three weeks of June). Trends for 1986-99 are average annual rates of change shown by sample populations. Significance of trends (t-test) indicated as: n.s. not significant, ** P < 0.01, *** P < 0.001). Further details of calculation of trends are given in section 1.2.2.

3.23.1a Counts of birds in study plots. Figures are summed means of 5-10, or exceptionally [4], annual counts of study plots.

	NW Scotland	Shetland	NE Scotland	SE Scotland	Wales
1986-99 annual % change	+1.0 n.s.	+0.1 n.s.	+5.1***	+3.1***	+5.3***
1999	3,407	11,306	3,332	5,394	10,410
2000	3,506	12,235	3,372	7,264	10,338
1999-2000 % change	+2.9[a]	+8.2[b]	+1.2[c]	+34.7[d]	-0.7[e]

Colonies: [a] Handa; [b] Hermaness, Sumburgh Head, Burravoe, Eshaness, Noss, Troswick Ness, Fair Isle; [c] Fowlsheugh; [d] Isle of May, St. Abb's Head; [e] South Stack, Skomer, Skokholm, Stackpole NNR, Elegug Stacks.

3.23.1b Counts of whole common guillemot colonies. Note that whole-colony counts should be treated with some caution as the numbers of birds attending colonies may vary markedly from day to day. Replicate study plot counts are better indicators of population change. Trends given for SE Scotland are whole-colony counts for the Isle of May, those for NE England are whole-colony counts at the Farne Islands, those for Wales are whole-colony counts at Skomer, Skokholm, Stackpole and Elegug Stacks and those for NW England are whole-colony counts at St. Bee's Head.

	SE Scotland	NE England	Wales	SW England	NW England/ I. of Man
1986-99 annual % change	+3.4**	+4.7***	+5.1***	-	+1.3 n.s.
1999	29,632	31,386	28,396	1,259	8,251
2000	36,089	33,038	28,767	1,679	8,643
1999-2000 % change	+21.8[a]	+5.3[b]	+1.3[c]	+33.4[d]	+4.8[e]

Colonies: [a] Isle of May, Inchkeith, Craigleith, The Lamb, Bass Rock; [b] Farne Islands; [c] Stackpole Head plus Elegug Stacks and nearby, Skokholm, Skomer, Grassholm, Penbwchdy, Caldey, Yns Ddu, Pen Brosh, Ramsey Island, St. Margaret's Island, Bardsey, Ynys Gwylan; [d] St. Aldhelm's - Durlston, Berry Head (peak June count); [e] St. Bees Head, Peel Hill.

In Orkney, a series of monitoring plots at five mainland colonies was counted in 2000 as part of the JNCC triennial monitoring scheme. Numbers of birds in these plots were 3.8% higher overall than in 1997. Increases were recorded at all plots, though the only significant increase was at Mull Head (+5.1%, t=2.568, d.f. =9, P<0.05). Non-significant increases were 3.9% at Costa Head, 3.5% at Marwick Head, 2.8% at Row Head and 1.1% at Gultak. Whole colony counts at Costa Head and Mull Head produced 9,630 and 1,974 birds respectively. Compared to similar previous counts, these represent increases of 28.5% at Costa Head since 1985, and 23.9% at Mull Head since 1991.

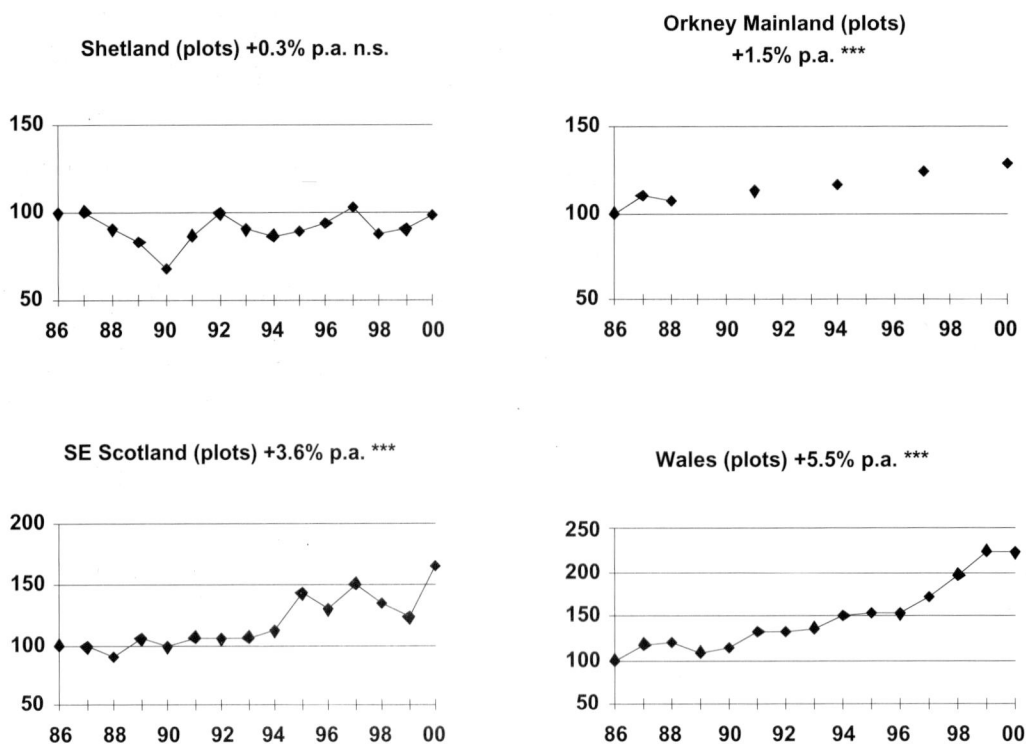

Figure 3.23.1 Population indices for breeding common guillemots in various regions, 1986-2000. Indices are derived from counts of adults in June. Trends for 1986-2000 are average annual rates of change shown by sample populations. Significance of trends indicated as: n.s. not significant, *** P < 0.001. Further details of calculation of trends are given in section 1.2.2.

In north-west Scotland, there was a non-significant increase at sample plots on Handa (+2.9%). Elsewhere in the region, numbers on the south-east coast of Rum also increased, up 14.6% to 2,325.

Breeding success (Table 3.23.2)

The intensity of monitoring at the colonies listed in Table 3.22.2 varies and this may affect estimates of breeding success (Walsh *et al.* 1995). Direct comparisons between colonies are therefore inadvisable without prior consultation with the authors. It was generally a reasonable season in 2000, with only four out of ten colonies recording below average breeding success. Average breeding success across the ten monitored colonies was 0.74 chicks fledged per breeding pair, above the 1986-99 mean of 0.73 (s.e. ± 0.01) across between three and 15 colonies monitored annually.

The monitored colony at North Sutor (north Scotland) had an improved breeding season, though success of 0.61 was still well below average (1994-99 mean 0.72, s.e. ± 0.04). A similar pattern was observed at the Isle of May; breeding success was 0.73 chicks per laying pair, but was still below the mean for the previous 19 seasons (95% confidence interval 0.78-0.82). Fledgling weights were closer to the long term mean, and losses during the chick period dropped to 8% (cf. 19% in 1999), closer to that typically recorded prior to 1998 (5-6%) (Bull *et al.* 2000).

In Orkney, breeding success of 0.79 was the highest on record for Mull Head (1989-99 mean 0.71, s.e. ± 0.02), but success of 0.68 was below average for the west coast colony of Marwick Head (1986-99 mean 0.73, s.e. ± 0.02).

In Shetland, as was the case in 1999, productivity at the sheltered Sumburgh Head study plot did not reflect the general situation. An estimated 8,000-9,000 chicks were washed into the sea along the west side of Sumburgh Head during the storm on 13 June, which occurred too late in the breeding season for pairs to relay (Heubeck 2000). However, on Fair Isle, common guillemots had an average breeding season producing 0.75 chicks per active site. On Handa (Sutherland), productivity of 0.74 per pair was above average (1988-99 mean 0.69, s.e. $\pm$ 0.02). In Wales, the productivity on Skomer was 0.63 chicks per site. This was the lowest value recorded at this site, well below the 1989-99 mean of 0.74 (s.e. $\pm$ 0.02), and again lower than that found by Sheffield University, which was on a par with last year s figure (Brown & Easton 2000). In south-west England, common guillemots at Durlston Head had an excellent season with an above average productivity of 0.87 (1993-99 mean 0.83, s.e. $\pm$ 0.02).

Table 3.23.2 Common guillemot breeding success, 1999-2000 and colony averages: estimated number of chicks fledged per site regularly occupied by a pair or per pair laying. Superscript figures for individual colonies are numbers of study plots, figures are mean and standard error across all plots.

Colony	Colony average 1986-99			1999 chicks fledged/pair			2000 chicks fledged/pair			1999-2000
	Years	Mean	$\pm$s.e.	Sites^n	Mean	$\pm$s.e.	Sites^n	Mean	$\pm$s.e.	Change
Handa	12	0.69	$\pm$0.02	219^3	0.60	$\pm$0.03	185^3	0.74	$\pm$0.02	+0.14
Sumburgh Head	11	0.67	$\pm$0.03	128^1	0.67	-	141^1	0.70	-	+0.03
Fair Isle	13	0.75	$\pm$0.01	168^2	0.79	$\pm$0.02	148^2	0.75	$\pm$0.04	-0.04
Papa Westray	11	0.70	$\pm$0.04	264^1	0.70	-	-	-	-	-
Marwick Head	13	0.73	$\pm$0.02	86^1	0.69	-	73^1	0.68	-	-0.01
Mull Head	10	0.71	$\pm$0.02	102^1	0.70	-	103^1	0.79	-	+0.09
North Sutor	6	0.72	$\pm$0.04	122^1	0.52	-	87^1	0.61	-	+0.09
Isle of May	14	0.79	$\pm$0.01	870^5	0.66	$\pm$0.01	$1,012^5$	0.73	$\pm$0.02	+0.07
Durlston	5	0.83	$\pm$0.02	-	-	-	62^1	0.87	-	-
Skokholm	4	0.87	$\pm$0.05	-	-	-	112^1	0.87	-	-
Skomer	11	0.74	$\pm$0.01	242^5	0.65	$\pm$0.05	225^5	0.63	$\pm$0.08	-0.02
Total $^{\text{no colonies}}$	-	-	-	$2,201^9$	0.66	$\pm$0.02	$2,148^{10}$	0.74	$\pm$0.03	$+0.05^8$

3.24 Razorbill *Alca torda*

Breeding numbers (Table 3.24.1, Figure 3.24.1)

Tables 3.24.1a and 3.24.1b show overall regional changes in razorbill numbers for sample plots and at whole colonies from 1999 to 2000. Generally, multiple plot counts are preferred for monitoring annual population changes in razorbills as they smooth out day-to-day fluctuations in numbers of birds attending breeding colonies. It should also be noted that, because of their nesting habits, razorbills are difficult to census, particularly in large colonies, and that consequently there may be considerable variation in counts between individual observers.

As with guillemots, mean numbers of adult razorbills attending sample plots varied between regions from 1999 to 2000. In Shetland, numbers increased at Sumburgh Head (+3.6%), Eshaness (+0.5%), Troswick Ness (+18.8%), Hermaness (+24.3%) and Noss (+6.5%), though none were significant. Non-significant decreases occurred at Burravoe (-2.4%) and Fair Isle (-1.0%). Whole colony counts revealed an increase of 26.7% (617) at Hermaness since the previous comparable June count in 1994. However, counts done in early May, during the early morning and in the evening when birds are thought to be more visible outside their nest entrances (Walsh *et al.* 1995), totalled 1,343. On Fair Isle, a whole colony count of 3,599 represented an increase of 9.2% since 1998. However, the razorbill population on Foula still appears to be in a long-term decline as a whole colony count recorded a minimum of 2,121 birds, compared with 6,170 in 1987 and 10,373 in 1976.

Table 3.24.1 Population changes at monitored razorbill colonies, 1998-2000 (adults attending colony in first three weeks of June unless otherwise indicated). Regional totals of fewer than 50 birds are excluded. Trends for 1986-99 are average annual rates of change shown by sample populations. Significance of trends indicated as: n.s. not significant, * P < 0.05, ** P < 0.01, *** P < 0.001. Further details of calculation of trends are given in section 1.2.2.

3.24.1a Counts of birds in study plots. Figures are based on the means of 5-10, exceptionally [4], annual counts of study plots within each colony.

	NW Scotland	Shetland	NE Scotland	SE Scotland	Wales
1986-99 annual % change	-	+1.4 n.s.	+1.3 n.s.	+4.6***	+3.9***
1999	534	585	200	1,051	2,005
2000	497	614	306	1,121	2,073
1999-00 % change	-6.9[a]	+5.0[b]	+53.0[c]	+6.7[d]	+3.4[e]

Colonies: [a] Handa; [b] Sumburgh Head, Noss, Hermaness, Eshaness, Burravoe, Troswick Ness, Fair Isle; [c] Fowlsheugh; [d] Isle of May, St. Abb's Head; [e] Skomer, Skokholm, Elegug Stacks, Stackpole NNR, South Stack.

3.24.1b Single counts of whole colonies. Trends given for Wales are whole-colony counts at Skomer, Skokholm, Stackpole and Elegug Stacks and those for NW England are whole-colony counts at St. Bee's Head.

	Isle of May (birds)	Other SE Scotland (sites)	NE England (sites)	Wales	NW England & Isle of Man
1986-99 annual % change	+6.4***	-	-	+1.7***	+1.6 n.s.
1999	3,786	440	146	5,590	312
2000	3,958	555	174	6,467	215
1999-00 % change	+4.5	+26.1[a]	+19.2[b]	+15.7[c]	-31.1[d]

Colonies: [a] Inchcolm, Inchkeith, Craigleith, Fidra, The Lamb, Bass Rock; [b] Farne Islands; [c] Stackpole Head plus Elegug Stacks and nearby, Skokholm, Skomer, Grassholm, St. Margaret's Island, Caldey, Yns Ddu, Pen Brush, Yns Gwylan; [d] St. Bees Head.

In Orkney, sample plot counts were carried out at five mainland colonies as part of the JNCC triennial monitoring scheme. Overall numbers increased by 6.6% since 1997. Significant increases were recorded at Row Head (26.6%, t=2.249, d.f. =11, P<0.05) and Mull Head (10.0%, t=2.691, d.f. =9, P<0.05) with non-significant increases occurring at Gultak (+16.7%) and Marwick Head (+1.8%). A non-significant decrease occurred at Costa Head (-9.9%). Whole colony counts at Mull Head and Costa Head totalled 189 and 648 respectively.

In south-east Scotland, plot counts increased non-significantly on the Isle of May by 4.0%, but there was a significant increase of 21.6% at St. Abb s Head (t=3.956, d.f. =11, P<0.01). A whole-colony count of the Isle of May found a total of 3,958 birds, 4.5% more than in 1999. At Fowlsheugh in north-east Scotland, there was a significant increase of 52.6% in plot counts (t=5.211 d.f. =8, P<0.001). In north-east England, numbers increased on the Farnes to 174 sites (146 in 1999).

Shetland
(plots) +1.8% p.a. n.s.

North-east Scotland
(Fowlsheugh plots) +2.3% p.a. *

South-east Scotland
(plots) +4.6% p.a. ***

Wales
(plots) +3.6% p.a. ***

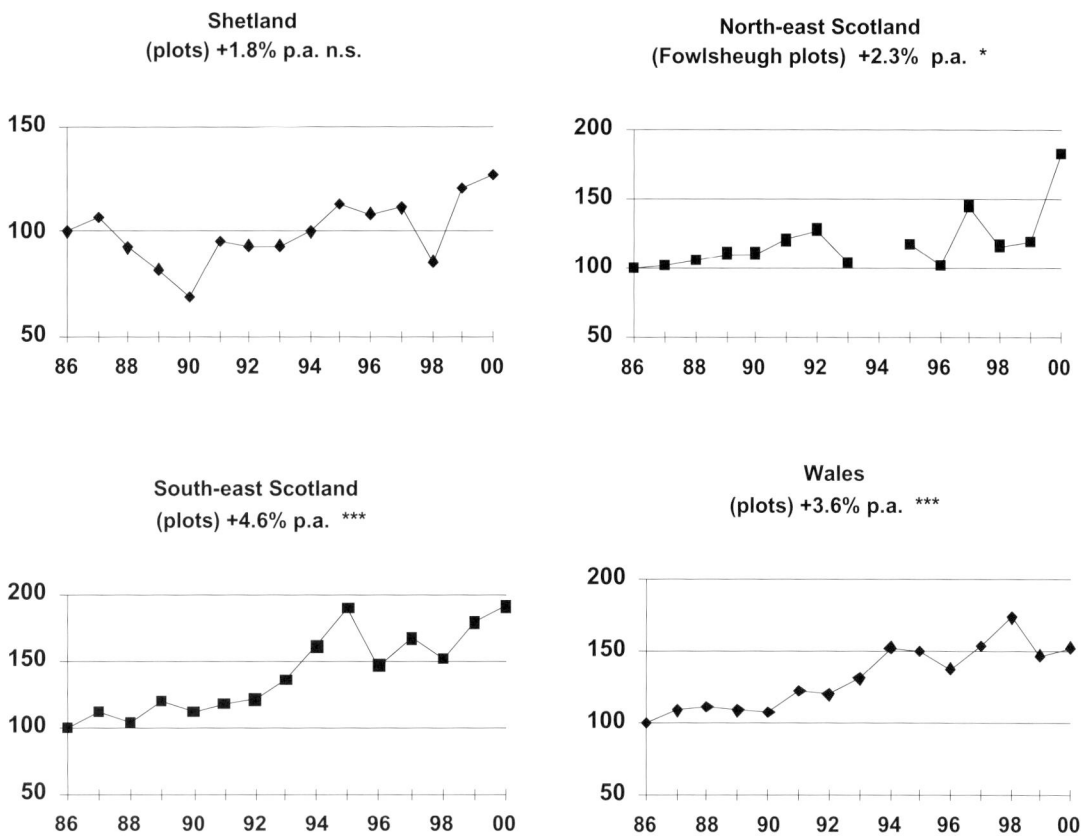

Figure 3.24.1 Population indices for breeding razorbills in various colonies and regions, 1986-2000. Trends for 1986-2000 are average annual rates of change shown by sample populations. Significance of trends indicated as: n.s. not significant, * P<0.05, *** P<0.001. Further details of calculation trends are given in section 1.2.2.

The largest proportional increase in Wales between 1999 and 2000 was on Skomer, where numbers increased by 32.6%, to 3,894 birds. An increase was also evident on Skokholm (+5.6% to 1,246 birds). Declines in whole colony counts were noted at St. Margaret s (-61.8% to 44 birds) following an increase between 1998 and 1999, and Stackpole Head (-25.0% to 93 birds). There was a significant increase in sample plot counts on Skomer (+24.9%, t=4.165, d.f. =15, P<0.001) and at Skokholm (+11.8%, t=2.130, d.f. =18, P<0.05) and non-significant decreases were recorded in sample plots on Stackpole (-30.1%) and Elegug Stacks (-9.0%). At South Stack there was a non-significant decrease of 13.9%. The trend of razorbill populations in Wales contrasts with that of common guillemot. Counts of monitored study plots and whole colonies show razorbills are increasing, whereas common guillemots have decreased at study plots, and increases at whole colony counts in 2000 are less than the annual average.

In north-west England, numbers decreased from 1999 at St. Bees Head by 19.6%, to 251 birds. In north-west Scotland, numbers on the south-east coast of Rum declined by 69.4% to 61.

Breeding success (Table 3.24.2)

It should be noted that the intensity of monitoring at the colonies listed in Table 3.24.2 varies and that this may affect estimates of breeding success (Walsh *et al*. 1995). Direct comparisons between colonies are therefore inadvisable without prior consultation with the authors.

Mean breeding success at six colonies monitored in 2000 was 0.60 (s.e. ± 0.05) chicks fledged per breeding pair, significantly lower than the 1986-99 mean of 0.70 (s.e. ± 0.01) measured in between one and six colonies annually. The breeding success at four colonies (Fair Isle, North Sutor, Farne

Islands and Skomer) was the lowest on record. On Fair Isle (Shetland), mean breeding success was only 0.47 chicks fledged per egg, well below the 1991-99 average of 0.63 (s.e. $\pm$ 0.04). At the small colony of North Sutor (Easter Ross), breeding success in 2000 was 0.64, compared with the 1997-99 mean 0.82, s.e. $\pm$ 0.03. Similarly, at the Farnes, breeding success of 0.54 was well below the long-term average (1996-99 mean 0.70, s.e. $\pm$ 0.02).

On the Isle of May, breeding success averaged 0.68 young fledged per pair, an increase after the low figure recorded in 1999 (0.52), and close to the 1986-99 mean of 0.69 (s.e. $\pm$ 0.02). In Wales, breeding success varied between the two reporting colonies. On Skomer, only 0.48 chicks fledged per pair compared with the 1993-99 mean of 0.63, s.e. $\pm$ 0.03. However, productivity was higher on Skokholm (0.81), though lower than average for this site (1995-98 mean 0.86, s.e. $\pm$ 0.04).

Table 3.24.2 Razorbill breeding success, 1999-2000: estimated number of chicks fledged per site regularly occupied by a pair or per pair laying. Superscript figures for individual colonies are numbers of study plots. Where three or more study plots are monitored, colony figures are mean and standard error across all plots.

Colony	Colony average 1986-99			1999 chicks fledged/pair			2000 chicks fledged/pair			1999-2000 change	
	Years	Mean	$\pm$s.e.	Sites^n	Mean	$\pm$s.e.	Sites^n	Mean	$\pm$s.e.	Mean	$\pm$s.e.
Fair Isle	9	0.63	$\pm$0.04	59^1	$\leq$0.51	-	86^1	0.47	-	-0.04	-
North Sutor	3	0.82	$\pm$0.03	19^1	0.79	-	22^1	0.64	-	-0.15	-
Isle of May	14	0.69	$\pm$0.02	142^4	0.52	$\pm$0.06	149^4	0.68	$\pm$0.05	+0.16	-
Farnes	4	0.70	$\pm$0.02	37^1	0.65	-	24^1	0.54	-	-0.11	-
Skokholm	4	0.86	$\pm$0.04	-	-	-	70^1	0.81	-	-	-
Skomer	7	0.63	$\pm$0.03	311^5	0.56	$\pm$0.06	223^5	0.48	$\pm$0.03	-0.08	-
Total [no. colonies]	-	-	-	568^5	0.61	$\pm$0.05	574^6	0.60	$\pm$0.05	-0.04^5	$\pm$0.05

3.25 Black guillemot *Cepphus grylle*

Breeding numbers (Table 3.25.1)

Unless otherwise stated, all figures refer to early morning spring counts of individuals in adult plumage (Walsh *et al*. 1995). In Shetland, there was an overall increase of 9.5% in sample areas surveyed in both 1999 and 2000. This increase may be at least partly due to the fact that most sites were only counted once in 1999, but also because the higher of two counts was used for all sites in 2000. The monitoring plot on the east coast of Fetlar showed a 21.5% increase in numbers between 1999 and 2000. A whole-island survey of Noss found 112 breeding adults, identical to 1999, but 21.1% down on the previous count in 1994. On the west side of Shetland, monitored colonies along the coast affected by the *Braer* oil spill in 1993 declined slightly, as did numbers on Foula. On Fair Isle, numbers on the east coast showed a 20.1% increase on 1999, though numbers at the Busta Geo boulder beach continue to fall possibly due to predation by domestic cats.

In Orkney, 476 birds were counted at North Ronaldsay, representing an increase of 26.3% on 1999. On Papa Westray, 130 birds were counted at North Hill and Holm of Papay. This represents declines of 25.3% and 38.4% respectively on 1999 counts, continuing long-term declines recorded at each site since 1991. On the west coast of Scotland, a count of 220 birds on Eigg constituted a 46.7% increase since the last complete count in 1996. On the Isle of Man, after two years of increases, the number of birds at Peel Hill decreased by 29.9% to 108 individuals, a similar level to the 1997 count (101 birds).

Table 3.25.1 Population changes at monitored black guillemot colonies, 1999-2000 (adults in breeding habitat in early morning, late March-early May). Trends for periods indicated are average annual rates of change shown by sample populations. Significance of trends indicated as: n.s. not significant, * P < 0.05. For further details of the calculation of these trends see section 1.2.2. The figures for Fetlar (east coast) differ from Thompson *et al.* 1999), as first-year birds have been excluded.

	Fair Isle (east coast)	Fetlar (east coast)	Foula (N & S coasts)	Braer coast Shetland	Other Shetland	Isle of Man
Annual % change (period covered)	-2.9* (1986-99)	+0.5 n.s. (1987-99)	-	+3.6* (1993-99)	-	+2.4* (1986-99)
1999	144	209	159	219	499	154 (late)
2000	173	254	156	215	532	108
1999-2000 % change	+20.1	+21.5	-1.9	-1.8[a]	+6.6[b]	-29.9

Colonies: [a] Kettlaness, West Burra, [b] Lunning, Noss north coast, Hillswick Ness, Tingon east; [c] Peel Hill.

Breeding success

Very few data were collected in 2000. On Fair Isle, breeding success averaged 1.07 chicks fledged per nest from a small sample of 15 sites, well above the 1988-99 mean of 0.79 (s.e. ± 0.07). For the third successive year, no sites were found in the boulder beaches in the south-east corner of the island, where domestic cats are thought to have been responsible for the desertion of several traditional sites. Elsewhere in Shetland, a check of ten sites in the Fore Holm (Scalloway) colony in late July, when chicks should have been near to fledging, found only one large young. All other chicks were small and obviously the result of clutches that had been relayed after losses during the June storm (Okill 2000). On Foula, no sites were monitored, though several known nesting pairs appeared not to have chicks or eggs after the June storm. In Orkney, average clutch/brood size in 32 nests checked on Auskerry in mid July was 1.53 (including three nests that failed), compared to 1.35, 1.43, 1.07 and 1.22 in the previous four years. On North Ronaldsay, the average number of young in nests located for ringing was 1.76, well above the average recorded since 1996 (1.46, s.e. ± 0.06). In western Scotland, mink once again caused breeding failure at several sites (Craik 2000). In Ireland, approximately one chick fledged per nest from 25 monitored nests on Old Lighthouse Island, which was average for this site (1986-99 mean 1.0, s.e. ± 0.09). On Rockabill, a total of 37 nests fledged an average of 1.24 chicks. In Wales, two well-grown chicks were found in June on Ynys Gwylan Fawr, near Bardsey. This was the first time the species had nested on the island and occurred after an apparent spread from the established breeding site on Puffin Island, Anglesey. Nesting attempts also took place at several other locations in this area (Stansfield 2000).

3.26 Atlantic puffin *Fratercula arctica*

Breeding numbers

Few data were collected in 2000. On Fair Isle, counts were made of birds visible on land or in the sea and air adjacent to the colony on several evenings in late April and early May. A total of 15,118 birds were seen, 13% lower than in 1995. The raw counts of birds on land were also used to derive a total population estimate by application of a correction factor based on the proportion of a study group of colour-ringed birds at the Roskilie colony visible during the main count periods. The resultant population estimate of 80,000 birds would represent a 100% increase on the 1995 estimate. However, this estimate may be too high as the presence of great skuas in the Roskilie colony may have resulted in a lower proportion of colour-ringed birds being visible than would be typical of other areas (Shaw *et al.* 2000). On Foula, an evening count of birds ashore in early June recorded 13,261

Individuals. Using a correction factor, similar to those used at Hermaness and Fair Isle, to convert the number of individuals to breeding pairs provides an estimate for the Foula population in the order of 20,000-25,000 pairs (Harvey *et al.* 2000). This suggests a substantial decline since 1987 when the population totalled almost 48,000 apparently occupied burrows. In south-west Scotland, 2,659 birds were counted on Lunga. In south-east Scotland, 1,373 birds were counted on Inchkeith, similar to the figure counted there in 1998. On Handa in north-west Scotland, there was an increase in the area occupied on the main island. This follows initial recolonisation in 1999, which occurred after a successful rat eradication programme in 1997 (Stoneman 2000). In Wales, the peak spring count on Skomer was 10,614 birds, the highest recorded since 1993. On Skokholm a peak spring count of 3,092 birds was within the range recorded there over the previous five years. On Ynys Gwylan Fawr, 1,113 occupied burrows were counted. This represents an increase of 112% on the 1999 count of 524 occupied burrows and far exceeds previous counts (386 in 1993, 457 in 1998). In north-west Ireland, evening flights of between 150 and 250 birds were seen heading toward Buddagh Island, potentially, a new colony.

Breeding success (Table 3.26.1)

Productivity was better than in 1999 at the majority of monitored colonies, though still below the long-term average for most. Breeding success on the Isle of May was 0.73 chicks fledged per egg laid, slightly below the 1986-99 average (0.77, s.e. $\pm$ 0.03). Productivity on the Farnes in 2000 increased to 0.77 chicks per egg laid, the highest recorded since 1996 and above the 1994-99 average of 0.71 (s.e. $\pm$ 0.08).

Table 3.26.1 Atlantic puffin breeding success, 1999-2000: estimated number of chicks fledged per egg or occupied burrow (Welsh colonies). Superscript indicates number of colonies.

Colony	1999 chicks fledged/pair				2000 chicks fledged/pair				1999-2000 change	
	Burrows	Range	Mean	$\pm$s.e.	Burrows	Range	Mean	$\pm$s.e.	Mean	$\pm$s.e.
Fair Isle	68	-	0.63	-	64	-	0.58	-	-0.05	-
Isle of May	181	-	0.58	-	182	-	0.73	-	+0.15	-
Farne Islands	100	-	0.64	-	100	-	0.77	-	+0.13	-
Skomer	88	-	0.70	-	69	-	0.75	-	+0.05	-
Total	437[4]	0.58-0.70	0.64	$\pm$0.02	415[4]	0.58-0.77	0.71	$\pm$0.04	+0.07[4]	$\pm$0.05

In Shetland, breeding success was poor on Fair Isle, averaging 0.58 chicks per egg laid, well below the 1986-99 mean (0.73, s.e. $\pm$ 0.02). This equalled the low value recorded in 1998: during the previous 13 seasons only 1990, when 0.57 chicks fledged per egg laid, has been a poorer year. In Wales, breeding success on Skomer averaged 0.75 chicks fledged per occupied burrow, slightly below the long-term mean of 0.77 (s.e. $\pm$ 0.02). On Ynys Gwylan Fawr, a sample of 44 accessible burrows was monitored over two visits, from which 34 large young were ringed and ten failed. Assuming all chicks fledged, productivity would equal 0.77.

4 Acknowledgements

We are very grateful to the following for their assistance with the monitoring of seabirds in Britain and Ireland in 2000 and to Jim Reid, Kate Thompson, Clive Craik, Keith Gillon, Robin Sellers and Sarah Wanless for their helpful comments on drafts of this report. Sincere apologies to any observers inadvertently omitted.

B. Adam, M. Adam, R.G. Adam, M. Adcock, D. Aiton, P. Akers, B. Allen, D. Allen, G. Allison, B. Anderson, D.J. Andrews, T. Appleton, E. Archer, M. Archer, J. Auber, S. Ayres,T. Bagworth, Bardsey Bird & Field Observatory, R. Barrett, C. Bartholomew, T. Begg, S. Benn, L. Berry, T. Best, BirdWatch Ireland, T.R. Birkhead, M. Blankers, M.A. Blick, S.P. Botham, C.J. Booth, O. Breffit, T. Bridge, I. Brockway, J.G. Brown, T. Brown, W. Bruce, F. Buchler, J. Bull, I. Bullock, A. Burrows, S. Butler, D. Butterfield, J. Cadbury, Calf of Man Bird Observatory, J. Callion, M. Carrier, P. Catchpole, A. Carter, L. Cavill, Centre for Ecology and Hydrology, P. Charlton, J. Chester, D. Chown, G. Churchill, H. Clarke, C. Cockburn, R. Coleman, P.N. Collin, Conwy County Borough Council, M. Cook, D. Cooper, R. Cooper, Copeland Bird Observatory, D. Cormack, Countryside Council for Wales, R. Cox, J.C.A. Craik, A. Crawford, A.J. Crease, S. Croft, J. Crook, O. Crowe, Cumbria Wildlife Trust, R. Cussen, S.R.D. da Prato, P. Davey, J. Davies, P.E. Davis, D. de Palacio, A. de Potier, P. Detheridge, I. Dillon, Dorset County Council, A. Dudney, T. Dudney, A. Duncan, R. Duncan, T. Dunn, Durlston Country Park, East of Scotland Tern Conservation Group, J. Easton, Edward Grey Institute, G.R. Ekins, M. Ellison, English Nature, Environment Agency, Essex Wildlife Trust, P. Ellis, D. Evans, Fair Isle Bird Observatory Trust, K. Fairclough, K. Ferry, S. Finney, P. Fisher, D. Fletcher, Forth Seabird Group, J. Fowler, I. Francis, R. Fraser, M. Freeman, M. Furness, R.W. Furness, S. Furness, O. Gabb, B. Gardner, J. Gear, S. Gear, M. Gee, K. Gillham, Glasgow University Applied Ornithology Unit, J. Glazebrook, R. Gomes, P.R. Gordon, A. Graham, K. Graham, Grampian Ringing Group, R. Griffiths, K. Hague, S. Hales, G. Hall, E. Hamler, A. Harding, N. Harding, R. Harold, M.P. Harris, P. Harvey, R. Harvey, V. Harvey, L. Hatton, R.J. Haycock, V. Heaney, D. Hemsley, Highland Ringing Group, T. Hodge, A. Hogg, P. Hollinrake, P. Holmes, C.A. Holt, N. Holton, H. Hume, E. Humphreys, Industry Nature Conservation Association, S. James, D. Jardine, M. Jennings, A. Johnson, Joint Nature Conservation Committee St. Kilda Expedition, D. Jones, Kent Wildlife Trust, P. Kinnear, A. Knight, R. Lambert, Lancashire Wildlife Trust, D. Law, A. Leitch, V. Lewis, R. Lidstone-Scott, A. Little, B. Little, K. Little, S. Little, N. Littlewood, G. Lohore, R.M. Lord, Lothian Ringing Group, K. Luxford, B. McCurley, A. McGeehan, D. McGinn, D. McGrath, N. McKee, E. Macleod, H. E. Maggs, M. Maher, R. Macklin, A. Maljkovic, M. Marsh, T. Martin, A. Mathieson, E.R. Meek, M. Mellor, O.J. Merne, Merseyside Ringing Group, A. Miller, A. Mitchell, P.I. Mitchell, M. Moeller-Holtkamp, S. Money, A.S. Moore, A. Moralee, R. Morris, S. Morris, P. Morrison, S.J. Morrison, R.A. Morton, M. Moss, D. Moxom, G. Moyes, A. Murray, S. Murray, National Parks & Wildlife Service (Ireland), National Trust, National Trust for Scotland, M. Newell, V. Newes, S. Newton, North Wales Wildlife Trust, North Ronaldsay Bird Observatory, D. Offer, J.D. Okill, M. Oksien, P. Oliver, E. Olley, K. Orr, N. Oughtred, A. Parfitt, J. Partridge, K. Partridge, C.M. Perrins, K. Perry, S. Pfeiffer, B. Phalan, S. Pidcock, B.J. Pinchen, R. Plowman, P. Porter, D. Powell, , G. Pullan, E. Rainey, A.D.K. Ramsay, B. Ramsay, N. Ratcliffe, G.W. Rebecca, J. Reed, A. Reid, K.J. Rideout, A. Robinson, K. Robinson, P. Robinson, B. Robson, C. Rodger, M. Rooney, M. Rudge, S. Russell, D.. Russell, Sanda Ringing Group, B. Sansom, A. Sapsford, Scottish Natural Heritage, Scottish Wildlife Trust, The Seabird Group, R.M. Sellers, D.N. Shaw, S. Shaw, Shetland Ringing Group, A. Skene, D. Slessor, C. Smith, M. Smith, R. Smith, S. Smith, South Holderness Countryside Society, D.J. Sowter, A. Speer, M. Spencer, S. Spray, G. Stamp, S. Stansfield, M. Stephenson, L. Stewart, U. Stoneman, Strangford Lough Wildlife Scheme, Suffolk Wildlife Trust, T.M. Sunderland, S. Sutcliffe, J. Swale, T. Swandale, D. Swann, R.L. Swann, Tain Royal Academy Bird Group, Talisman Energy, M. Tasker, Tees Ringing Group, C. Temple, D.A. Thompson, G. Thompson, I. Thompson, J. Thompson, R. Thorne, M. Thornton, R. Thorpe, H. Towll, S. Travis, Treshnish Isles Auk Ringing Group, P. Troake, G. Tyler, A.J. Upton, B. Uttley, B. Wainwright, J. Walker, S. Walker, P.M. Walsh, J. Walton, S. Wanless, R.M. Ward, A. Webb, S.J. White, M. Whitmore, A. Wight, The Wildlife Trust West Wales, C. Williams, E.J. Williams, J. Williams, S.J. Williams, S. Willis, F. Wilson, J. Wilson, M. Wilson, R. Wilson, E. Wiseman, K. Woodbridge, L. Woodrow, S. Woodward, A. Wright, B. Wright, M. Wright, A. Young, S. Young and B. Zonfrillo.

5. Bibliography

5.1 References used in this report.

Andrews, D.J., Thompson, D.A., Rainey, E. & Stewart, L. 2000. *Strangford Lough Wildlife Scheme Nesting Report 2000.* Unpublished report to the National Trust by the Strangford Lough Wildlife Scheme.

Avery, M.I., Burges, D., Dymond, N.J., Mellor, M., & Ellis, P.M. 1993. The status of Arctic terns *Sterna paradisaea* in Orkney and Shetland in 1989. *Seabird*, 15: 17-23.

British Ornithologists Union. 1992. Checklist of the Birds of Britain and Ireland. Tring, BOU.

Brown, J.G. & Easton, J. 2000. *Seabird monitoring on Skomer Island in 2000.* (Contractor: The Wildlife Trust, West Wales). Unpublished report to JNCC.

Bull, J., Wanless, S., & Harris, M.P. 2000. *Isle of May seabird studies in 2000.* (Contractor: Centre for Ecology and Hydrology) Unpublished report to JNCC.

Bullock, I. D. & Gomersall, C. H. 1981. The breeding populations of terns in Orkney and Shetland in 1980. *Bird Study,* 28: 187-200.

Coleman, R.J. 2001. *Breeding terns at St. Fergus Gas terminal, 2000.* Unpublished report, RSPB.

Craik, J.C.A. 2000. *Results of the Mink-Seabird Project in Year 2000.* Unpublished report.

Croft, S. & Marks, C. 1999. *The Breeding Performance of Arctic terns, Arctic Skuas and Great Skuas in Shetland and Orkney, 1999.* Unpublished RSPB report.

Crowe, O., Maljkovic, A. & Newton, S.F. 2000. Rockabill Tern Report 2000. *BirdWatch Ireland Conservation Report*, No. 00/2

Cramp, S., Bourne, W.R.P., & Saunders, D. 1974. The seabirds of Britain and Ireland. London, Collins.

Cramp, S. & Simmons, K.E.L. (Eds.) 1983. Handbook of the birds of Europe, the Middle East and North Africa: the birds of the Western Palearctic Vol. 3. Oxford, Oxford University Press.

Donald, P. & Bekhuis, J. 1993. In: The new atlas of breeding birds in Britain and Ireland: 1988-1991. Ed. By D.W. Gibbons, J.B. Reid and R.A. Chapman. London, Poyser.

Eden, P. 2000a. Weather log April 1999. Supplement to *Weather, 55(4).*

Eden, P. 2000b. Weather log May 1999. Supplement to *Weather, 55(5).*

Eden, P. 2000c. Weather log June 1999. Supplement to *Weather, 55(6).*

Eden, P. 2000d. Weather log July 1999. Supplement to *Weather, 55(7).*

Furness, R.W. 1997. *Skua survey in Hoy, June 1996.* (Contractor: Applied Ornithology Unit, University of Glasgow.) Unpublished report to Scottish Natural Heritage.

Furness, R. W. 2000. *Seabird studies on Foula, 2000.* Unpublished report, Applied Ornithology Unit, University of Glasgow.

Gilbert, G., Gibbons, D. W. & Evans, J. 1998b. Bird Monitoring Methods – a manual of techniques for key UK species. Great Britain, RSPB, BTO, JNCC, ITE & McCorquodale Confidential Print Ltd.

Gilbert G., Hemsley, D. & Shepherd, M. 1998b. A survey of Storm Petrels on the Treshnish Isles in 1996. *Scottish Birds,* 19: 145-153.

Harvey, P.V., Swale, J., Upton, A.J., Gear, S., Adam, M., Churchill, G., Gillham, K., & Skene, A. 2000. *A census of the seabirds of Foula – June 2000.* Unpublished report, Scottish Natural Heritage.

Heaney, V., Ratcliffe, N., Brown, A., Robinson, P.J. & Lock, L. The Status and Distribution of Storm Petrels and Manx Shearwaters on the Isles of Scilly. *In prep.*

Hemsley, D. 1999. *Studies of breeding birds and other biological recording on the Isle of May in 1999.* Unpublished report, Scottish Natural Heritage.

Heubeck, M. 2000. *SOTEAG ornithological monitoring programme 2000:summary report.* Unpublished report, University of Aberdeen.

James, P. C. & Robertson, H. A. 1985. The use of playback recordings to detect and census nocturnal burrowing seabirds. *Seabird*, 8: 18-20.

Jones, D. 2000. *Forth Islands bird report 2000.* Unpublished report, Forth Seabird Group.

Jones, S., Stamp, G., Graham, C., Hickling, J. 2000. *Little tern wardening at Gronant 2000.* Unpublished report, RSPB.

Lloyd, C., Tasker, M.L., & Partridge, K. 1991. *The status of seabirds in Britain and Ireland.* London, T. & A.D. Poyser.

Mead, C. & Wernham, C. 2000. *Erika* update. *The Seabird Group Newsletter*, No. 85: June 2000.

Meek, E. 2000. *Orkney seabird monitoring report 2000.* Unpublished report, RSPB.

Meek, E.R., Sim, I.M.W., & Ribbands, B. 1994. Breeding skuas in Orkney: the results of the 1992 census. *Seabird,* 16: 34-40.

Morton, R. 2000. *The breeding seabirds of Sanda 2000.* Unpublished report.

Murray, S. 2000. *A count of the Grassholm gannet colony from aerial photographs taken in 1999.* Unpublished report.

Murray, S. & Wanless, S. 1997. The status of the gannet in Scotland in 1994-95. *Scottish Birds,* 19: 10-27.

Newton, S., Mitchell, I. & Ross, B. 2000. The last frontier: a survey of nocturnal seabirds in Western Ireland and North Scotland. *BirdWatch Ireland Conservation Report,* No. 00/7.

Ogilvie, M. & the Rare Breeding Birds Panel. 2000. Rare breeding birds in the UK in 1998. *British Birds,* 93: 358-393.

Okill, J.D. 2000a. *Report to SOTEAG on red-throated divers in Shetland 2000.* Unpublished report, Shetland Ringing Group.

Okill, J.D. 2000b. *Report on seabirds in Shetland 2000.* Unpublished report, Shetland Ringing Group.

Okill, J.D. & Fowler, J.A. 2000. *Storm petrels on the Scalloway Islands.* Unpublished report, Shetland Ringing Group.

Perrins, C.M. 2000. *Skomer Island 2000 seabird survival studies* (Contractor: Edward Grey Institute of Field Ornithology.) Unpublished report to JNCC, Countryside Council for Wales and Wildlife Trust West Wales.

Ramsay, A.D.K. 2001. *Rum Manx shearwater report.* Unpublished report.

Ratcliffe, N., Vaughan, D. , Whyte, C. & Shepherd, M. 1998a. The status of storm petrels on Mousa, Shetland. *Scottish Birds*, 19: 154-159.

Ratcliffe N, D. Vaughan, C. Whyte & M. Shepherd 1998b. Development of playback census methods for storm petrels *Hydrobates pelagicus. Bird Study,* 45: 302-312

Robinson, P. & Colombé, S. 2000. *Roseate tern: species recovery programme, Isles of Scilly 2000.* Unpublished report, English Nature.

Rodger, C., 2000. *Hermaness and Keen of Hamar NNR annual report 2000.* Unpublished report, Scottish Natural Heritage.

Rideout, K.J., & Hall, G. 2000. *St. Abbs Head NNR seabird report 1999.* Unpublished report, National Trust for Scotland.

Sears, J., Ellis, P.M., Suddaby, D., & Harrop, H.R. 1995. The status of breeding Arctic skuas S*tercorarius parasiticus* and great skuas *S. skua* in Shetland in 1992. *Seabird, 17*: 21-31.

Sellers R.M. 2001, *Cormorant breeding colony survey- summary of 2000 counts.* Unpublished report, No. CBCS-R-019.

Shaw, D.N., Holt, C.A., Maggs, H.E. & de Palacio, D. 2000. *Fair Isle seabird studies 2000.* (Contractor: Fair Isle Bird Observatory). Unpublished report to JNCC.

Siokhin, V., Chernichko, I. & Ardamatskaya, T. 1988. Colonial-nesting waterbirds of the Ukraine. Akademia Nauk Ukraniskoj SSR, Kiev.

Smart, J. & Ratcliffe, N. 2000. *Monitoring the effectiveness of supplementary feeding as a means of reducing kestrel predation on little tern chicks at the Great Yarmouth colony.* Unpublished report, RSPB.

Smith, M. & Luxford, K. 2000. *Seabird studies in Fetlar 2000.* Unpublished report, RSPB.

Sowter, D.J. 2000. *The Tarnbrook Fell gullery report 2000.* Unpublished report.

Stansfield, S. 2000. *Seabird productivity monitoring for Ynys Enlli and Ynysoedd Gwylan in 2000.* Unpublished report to Bardsey Bird and Field Observatory.

Stone, B.H., Sears, J., Cranswick, P.A., Gregory, R.D., Gibbons, D.W., Rehfisch, M.M., Aebischer, N.J., & Reid, J.B. 1997. Population estimates of birds in Britain and in the United Kingdom. *British Birds,* 90: 1-22.

Stoneman, U. 2000. *Handa Island summer warden's report 2000.* Unpublished report, Scottish Wildlife Trust.

Swann, R.L. 2000a. *Canna seabird studies 2000.* (Contractor: Highland Ringing Group.) Unpublished report to JNCC.

Swann, R.L. 2000b. *Easter Ross seabird monitoring 2000.* Unpublished report, Highland Ringing Group.

Tasker, M. L., Moore, P. R. & Schofield, R. A. 1988. The Seabirds of St Kilda, 1987. *Scottish Birds*, 15: 21-29.

Thompson, K.R., Brindley, E., & Heubeck, M. 1997. *Seabird numbers and breeding success in Britain and Ireland, 1996.* Peterborough, Joint Nature Conservation Committee. (UK Nature Conservation, No. 21.).

Thompson, K.R., Pickerell, G., & Heubeck, M. 1999. *Seabird numbers and breeding success in Britain and Ireland, 1998.* Peterborough, Joint Nature Conservation Committee. (UK Nature Conservation, No. 23.).

Upton, A. J. & Maher, M. 2000. *Noss NNR annual report 2000.* Unpublished report, Scottish Natural Heritage.

Upton, A.J., Pickerell, G., & Heubeck, M. 2000. *Seabird numbers and breeding success in Britain and Ireland, 1999.* Peterborough, Joint Nature Conservation Committee. (UK Nature Conservation, No. 24.).

Walsh, P.M., Avery, M., & Heubeck, M. 1990. Seabird numbers and breeding success in 1989. *Nature Conservancy Council, CSD Report,* No. 1071.

Walsh, P.M., & Gordon, J.R.W. 1994. *Breeding status and population trends of lesser black-backed gulls* Larus fuscus, *herring gulls* L. argentatus *and great black-backed gulls* L. marinus *in the United Kingdom.* Unpublished report, Joint Nature Conservation Committee.

Walsh, P.M., Halley, D.J., Harris, M.P., del Nevo, A., Sim, I.M.W., & Tasker, M.L. 1995. *Seabird monitoring handbook for Britain and Ireland.* Peterborough, JNCC, RSPB, ITE, Seabird Group.

Walton, J. 2000. *Breeding birds of the Farne Islands 2000.* Unpublished report.

Wilkinson, L. 1990. SYSTAT: The system for statistics. SYSTAT Inc., Evanston.

Wilson, J. 2000. *Studies of breeding birds and other biological recording on the Isle of May in 2000.* Unpublished report, Scottish Natural Heritage.

Wilson, F., Thornton, M., Archer, E. & Newton, S.F. 2000. Kilcoole little tern report 2000. *BirdWatch Ireland Conservation Report*, No. 00/3.

5.2 Further reading relevant to breeding seabirds in Britain and Ireland published in 2000.

Caldow, R.W.G., & Furness, R.W. 2000. The effect of food availability on the foraging behaviour of breeding great skuas *Catharacta skua* and Arctic skuas *Stercorarius parasiticus. Avian Biology,* 31: 367-375.

Camphuysen, C.J. & Reid, J.B. (eds.) 2000. Seabird monitoring in Britain 1989-98: 10 years of the Seabird Monitoring Programme. *Atlantic Seabirds, Special Issue* 2: 97-244.

Craik, J.C. 2000. A simple and rapid method of estimating gull productivity. *Bird Study,* 47: 113-116.

Harris, M.P., Wanless, S., Rothery, P., Swann, R.L., & Jardine, D. 2000. Survival of adult common guillemots *Uria aalge* at three Scottish colonies. *Bird Study,* 47: 1-7.

Harris, M.P., Wanless, S., Webb, A. 2000. Changes in body mass of common guillemots *Uria aalge* in southeast Scotland throughout the year: implications for the release of cleaned birds. *Ringing & Migration,* 20: 134-142.

Mayhew, P., Chisholm, K., Insley, H., & Ratcliffe, N. 2000. A survey of storm petrels on Priest Island in 1999. *Scottish Birds,* 21: 78-84.

Phillips, R.A. & Hamer, K.C. 2000. Growth and provisioning strategies of Northern fulmars *Fulmarus glacialis. Ibis,* 142: 435-445.

Royle, N. 2000. Overproduction in the lesser black-backed gull – can marginal chicks overcome the initial handicap of hatching asynchrony? *Avian Biology,* 31: 335-344.